Also by Dr. Miriam Adahan:

EMETT:
Emotional Maturity Established Through Torah

It's All a Gift

Appreciating People
(Including Yourself)

Living with Difficult People
(Including Yourself)

Awareness

Thirty Seconds to Emotional Health

Miriam Adahan Handbooks
1. Nobody's Perfect
2. Living with Kids: Parents at Their Best
3. After the Chuppah
4. The Family Connection
5. Calm Down: Taking Control of Your Life

Dr. Miriam Adahan

Sticks *and* Stones
WHEN WORDS ARE USED AS WEAPONS

FELDHEIM PUBLISHERS
JERUSALEM • NEW YORK

First published 1998
Copyright © 1998 by Miriam Adahan
ISBN 0-87306-859-9

All rights reserved.
No part of this publication may be
translated, reproduced, stored in a retrieval
system or transmitted, in any form or by any
means, electronic, mechanical, photocopying,
recording, or otherwise, without permission in
writing from the publishers.

FELDHEIM PUBLISHERS
POB 35002 / Jerusalem, Israel

200 Airport Executive Park
Nanuet, NY 10954

10 9 8 7 6 5 4 3 2 1

Printed in Israel

בס"ד

מנחם אב, תשנ"ה

In this book, Miriam Adahan has done an important service for the Jewish community by calling attention to a problem that is often neglected out of ignorance: the problem of verbal abuse. Few are aware of the enormous harm that results from constant and abusive words, and fewer still are aware of the extent of the problem. The old adage we have heard when we were children, "Sticks and stones may break my bones but words will never harm me," is meant to divert attention from the perpetrators of verbal abuse. The statement itself could not be further from the truth, for sticks and stones break merely bones, but disrespectful words can break the soul.

This book will be of importance to the many people who give advice to distressed spouses, and perhaps call public attention to the social problem of verbal abuse. It may even convince a would-be abuser to avoid such destructive behavior. In addition, it gives advice, solace, sympathy and understanding to those who have suffered abusive marriages. Moreover, the book should succeed in bringing men and women in *chinuch* to discuss the severity of the *issur* of *ona'as devarim* and the harm that is caused by this *chet*. It can do much to effect a change of attitude and behavior in many future marriages.

Chaim Twerski

ACKNOWLEDGMENTS

I am very grateful to Mr. Yaakov Feldheim for his courage in publishing this book and, indeed, all my books, as they have sometimes stirred up controversy.

I am grateful to the Feldheim editorial staff as well, who bore with me patiently through many revisions.

I wish to thank Rabbi Uziel Weingarten, for his hundreds of extremely astute editorial comments.

But mostly, I am filled with gratitude to God, may His Name be blessed by all, for giving me the time and the desire to write this book, as well as all the various events which led me to recognize the extreme importance of having it published. Spending hours each day working on the subject has brought me to new heights of awareness and understanding.

We experience God's love for us as we express our love and respect for others. It is my fervent hope that all those who read this book will become more sensitive to the many ways it is possible to hurt other people's feelings, and that they will take extreme care to avoid doing so whenever possible.

This book may not reach those who need it the most, but the rest of us can accept upon ourselves a commitment to be more compassionate and speak more respectfully to people, no matter how much distress we may be in at the moment and regardless of the other person's status or behavior. In this way, each of us will bring greater *kedushah* [holiness] into the entire world.

CONTENTS

INTRODUCTION

Every person has two sides: one that seeks love and unity and fosters acts of kindness and sympathy; the other a destructive side which gives in to the urge to condemn, belittle and demean others and hate them for no reason, though we always give ourselves what seem like logical reasons based on race, creed, dress or behavior.

It is as if we all have a bit of the despot in us, thinking we have the right to judge who has worth and significance. The destructive part of us believes we have the right to show disrespect to those who do not meet our standards:

> "S/he's stupid (demanding, pampered, lazy, selfish, sloppy, boring, emotionally unstable, moody, etc.)! I can snub her."

> "S/he's rich (brilliant, beautiful, even-keeled, calm, popular and so highly accomplished)! She deserves my respect."

> "You're not brilliant and studious, so you're nothing. I can treat you like garbage."

> "You're not part of my group, so you don't count. You're invisible to me."

Hashem said, "Love your neighbor as yourself" (*Vayikra* 19:18). But most people have a very hard time putting this commandment into practice. Instead, we condemn family members, friends and strangers. We condemn with our eyes, our thoughts and sometimes our tongues. Some people are virtual "condemnaholics," constantly condemning everyone at any time. Like alcoholism, this addiction to criticism is very difficult to overcome.

The condemnatory mind develops very early in life. Around the age of three or four, many children are already taunting and excluding those who are different in any way. Many children, though quite charming at times, also torment peers or younger siblings for the sheer pleasure of doing so. Many never outgrow this tendency to belittle others and think it is normal and acceptable to do so when they become adults.

Human beings are transmitting stations, sending — and receiving — the most subtle messages. If one feels contempt for another, there is no way to avoid transmitting it, whether in speech or action. When scorn is expressed, whether to a child or an adult, it constitutes verbal abuse. My life is spent counseling people whose lives have been damaged by such abuse:

ೞ *A good friend of mine died a few months ago after a long struggle with cancer. Her youngest child, a ten-year-old, was playing with friends near her home recently when one of the girls suddenly shouted at her, "It's good that your mother died." The orphan had the presence of mind to say, "You should be happy that you have a mother," and then ran home, heartbroken. Already, being motherless meant being inferior to those who have mothers.*

ೞ *A woman cried about her teenage son, who locks himself in his bedroom for days at a time. He told her, "Since I'm not brilliant and don't learn well, I'm garbage." From the time he was little, his father has berated him mercilessly for not getting better marks. Recently, it was discovered that he* has learning disabilities. However, that didn't make him feel better. In his world, being a brilliant scholar is the only important thing. So now he feels he has no reason to live.

ᓚ A woman cried about her husband, "He keeps saying that I'm crazy and stupid. I keep house, work part-time every day in an old age home and take excellent care of my children. But he criticizes every little thing I do — how I dress, cook, clean, what I buy and even how I talk. If he keeps on like this, I will go crazy."

ᓚ A mother told me, "I just can't stop criticizing my children. I start attacking them from the time I wake up in the morning. This one doesn't get dressed fast enough. That one is dreaming instead of eating. The other one is still lying in bed after I've yelled at him a dozen times to get up. My husband can't do anything right in my eyes either. I'm destroying them and I can't stop." She, herself, was the product of a home in which criticism was distributed freely.

Thus, many people grow up thinking that those who are handicapped in any way, even merely learning-disabled or emotionally sensitive, are inferior, less entitled to live, less deserving of respect.

Obviously, we need to make judgments about people's character in issues concerning health, morality and Halachah. Other than that, making judgments is unnecessary and damaging.

Verbal abuse affects everyone. My hope is that this book will make people aware of when they are indulging in this terrible habit and, through awareness, be able to control themselves.

The tongue should be used to comfort, uplift and encourage others, not to cause pain. To love other people is considered the same as loving God (the *Shela Ha-kadosh, Sha'ar Ha-Osios*, 3). Love in turn brings peace.

"...If there is no peace, there is nothing" (Rashi, *Vayikra* 26:5). With our mouths, we can make peace or sow dissention. It is our choice. With the proliferation of various groups within the Jewish people, there is also a proliferation of discord and hatred between them. We are also witnessing the breakup of many families, so often due to the parents' failure to restrain the urge to criticize and condemn. In homes and schools, on playgrounds and in workplaces, hearts break and personal growth is stunted when people fail to speak compassionately and lovingly.

This trend can be reversed if we take seriously the words of our Sages:

"...JUDGE EVERY PERSON FAVORABLY"
• AVOS 1:6 •

"...BE OF THE DISCIPLES OF AARON, LOVING PEACE
AND PURSUING PEACE, LOVING YOUR FELLOW CREATURE
AND BRINGING THEM NEAR TO TORAH"
• AVOS 1:12 •

Only by fighting our own basest urges can we call ourselves true followers of Torah, people who sincerely strive to "love God and love His creations" (*Avos* 6:1) without excuses based upon group loyalty, momentary upsets or life disappointments, and regardless of others' status or behavior! (Of course, this does not apply to those who are truly evil or publicly acknowledged enemies of the Jewish people.)

Imagine what the world would be like if we all made a rule for ourselves: "I will not open my mouth unless I have love in my heart!" If we all try to put this into practice in our homes, we will be doing our part to improve the world.

A special note to parents
who are enstranged from their children:

After years of hostile enstrangement or a polite, but superficial relationship, an adult child may ask you to read this book and say, "The reason I am so distant from you is because of the *ona'as devarim* in our family. I've always felt so put down. I don't feel that I am accepted for who I am."

Your first response may be to fire back, "After all I've done for you! How dare you?" Or, "You are sinning! You are not showing respect for your parents!" The result will probably be more months or years of estrangement.

If you really want to have a relationship with your child, don't keep responding with, "After all I've done for you...." Instead, say, "I really care about what you have to say. I'm willing to listen to anything you want to tell me." Then listen!

You cannot have an honest relationship with a child who is never allowed to express his pain about what hurts him most. Few things are as painful as feeling unaccepted by a parent. Perhaps you were disappointed in him. Perhaps you wanted a child who was more successful, smarter, neater, more cooperative, etc.

You may not have realized how painful it was for your child to feel your disappointment, or think that another child was favored, or that you were so busy with your own interests or disappointments that you were unavailable. Whatever the problem, allow your child to speak honestly.

You might reply, "I made mistakes. I wasn't perfect." It's true. No parent is perfect. You have knowledge and sensitivity today that you did not have then. There may be information that the adult child can now handle about your own life and why you could not act differently twenty or thirty years ago.

By expressing your own feelings and listening to the feelings of your child now, your relationship will change. Your courage to be honest will, hopefully, bring out the emotional closeness which your child craves. That is the reason he is asking you to read this book — not to hurt you, but to heal old hurts so that you can both move on to a more loving relationship.

Recognizing
Ona'as Devarim

ONE

ONA'AS DEVARIM:
THE SOURCES

"DEATH AND LIFE ARE IN THE POWER OF THE TONGUE"
• MISHLEI 18:21 •

When God told Sarah that she would give birth to a child at the age of ninety (*Bereshis* 18:12-13), she expressed astonishment saying, "And my lord [husband] is so old?" When God retold this interchange to Avraham, He changed her words, telling Avraham, "Sarah laughed and said: 'How can this be when I am old?'" In other words, God Himself was careful not to hurt Avraham's feelings. This is how careful each of us must learn to be!

In contrast, it is common for children from English-speaking countries to hear the phrase, "Sticks and stones will break my bones, but words will never hurt me." This myth is so powerful that many people truly believe that they should not feel hurt when they are abused verbally. If they do feel hurt, they are castigated as being too sensitive, which makes the hurt even greater! How different this is from the Jewish way, in which we are told:

"LO SONU — DO NOT HURT OTHERS"
• VAYIKRA 25:17 •

Rashi explains that this refers to hurting others with words — *ona'as devarim*.

WHAT EXACTLY IS *ONA'AS DEVARIM*?

The Torah demands extreme sensitivity to others' feelings, as seen in numerous places, such as:

"DO NOT OPPRESS THE POOR, BLIND, THE ORPHAN,
WIDOW AND STRANGER"
• SHEMOS 22:20-23 •

"DO NOT SPEAK DISPARAGINGLY [*LASHON HARA*]
ABOUT YOUR FELLOWMAN"
• VAYIKRA 19:16 •

"DO NOT BE INDIFFERENT
TO YOUR FELLOWMAN'S SUFFERING"
• IBID. •

"DO NOT HATE YOUR BROTHER"
• IBID., 17 •

"DO NOT EMBARRASS YOUR FELLOWMAN"
• IBID. •

There is a general instruction in the Torah — "Walk in His ways" (*Devarim* 10:12) — which requires that a person be thoughtful, considerate, well-mannered and, in other words, a *mentsch*.

Two other places where *ona'ah* [deliberate hurting] is discussed are:

"DO NOT WRONG ONE ANOTHER"
• VAYIKRA 25:14 •

This refers to causing one pain in financial matters (*Bava Metzia* 58), such as an employer who does not pay his workers promptly; a borrower who does not repay a loan promptly; one who writes a check without bank coverage; a merchant who lies about the quality of his merchandise or charges exorbitant rates, etc.

"YOU SHALL NOT WRONG ONE ANOTHER,
BUT SHALL FEAR YOUR GOD..."
• VAYIKRA 25:17 •

This refers to hurting others with words. Rashi comments that intention is pivotal. In other words, *ona'as devarim* means a *deliberate* intention to hurt, mock, demean, demoralize, shame or undermine. *Bava Metzia* 58 provides examples of *ona'as devarim*:

❑ GETTING A PERSON'S HOPES UP UNNECESSARILY. For example, asking a storeowner how much an item costs when you have no intention of buying it.

❑ SHAMING A PERSON by reminding him of a defect he can do nothing about, such as telling him that he is ugly.

❑ ACTING OUT OF SPITE, as in sending a buyer on a wild-goose chase, telling him that another merchant has what he wants, knowing that the latter does not have it.

❑ HUMILIATING A PERSON, such as in reminding a *ba'al teshuvah* (one who has returned to a Torah way of life) of his previous immoral behavior.

❑ SHAMING A CONVERT because of his parents' behavior.

❑ SHAMING A PERSON WHO IS SUFFERING from an illness or tragedy, by saying, "It's your own fault," "This is a punishment from God," as Job's "friends" told him.

❑ CAUSING ONE'S WIFE TO CRY by speaking harshly to her.

Additional prohibitions are mentioned against:

❑ EMBARRASSING A PERSON by asking questions to which he may not know the answer (*Chullin* 6a).

❑ MENTIONING INFORMATION WHICH WILL CAUSE PEOPLE TO BECOME UNNECESSARILY NERVOUS or worried (*Pesachim* 4).

❑ SCOFFING at someone's merchandise (*Kesubos* 17).

❑ FRIGHTENING PEOPLE by getting enraged at them (*Sefer Yere'im* 170). [*Note*: The Rambam allows a parent to wear a superficial mask of anger in order to educate a child, *only* if the parent is in control of himself and does not really feel anger in his heart!]

❑ ACTING IN A MANNER WHICH DISGUSTS OTHERS, such as not bathing, spitting in people's presence, or giving a person charity in public (*Chagigah* 5).

There are endless ways to extrapolate from the above list. For example:

        ℣ Don't get a person's hopes up needlessly. A single man should not speak to a single woman in a way which makes her think he is interested in her when he is not.

        ℣ Don't shame others for traits over which they have no control. Do not shame a hyperactive or learning-disabled child by constantly telling him that he is stupid, clumsy, disorganized, impulsive or immature.

DO NOT TRIVIALIZE THE POWER OF THE TONGUE

According to the *Pele Yoetz*, any intentional act which causes pain to another is considered *ona'as devarim* (*Erech Ona'ah*). While we do not want to turn every unintentional slight into a major sin, we must be as careful as humanly possible not to hurt others:

"A HEALING TONGUE IS THE TREE OF LIFE, AND ONE WHO
DISTORTS IT WILL BE BROKEN IN THE WIND"
• MISHLEI 15:4 •

We are told that "Hashem will be an eternal light" (*Yeshayahu* 60:20), a fact which will be revealed only when the Jewish people are unified (*Midrash Tanchuma, Nitzavim* 1).

The Hebrew word for "respect" (*kavod*) implies "heaviness," i.e., to give weight or seriousness to people's feelings. This requires showing love and compassion and avoiding hatred and resentment toward our fellowman. Sadly, many define "fellowman" as only those belonging to one's narrow group, or only those who fulfill their expectations, thereby giving themselves blanket permission to speak angrily or condescendingly to everyone else.

It is all too easy to justify, excuse and rationalize hurtful behavior. At moments when we are unsure whether to say what is on the tip of our tongues, we should ask ourselves if what we are about to say "is good and righteous in the eyes of God" (*Devarim* 12:28, 13:19).

"SHAMING ANOTHER IN PUBLIC IS AKIN TO MURDER.
THE PAIN OF SHAME IS WORSE THAN DEATH"
• BAVA METZIA 58B •

Shaming anyone, in public or not, is a grave sin. Many

people mistakenly believe that *lashon hara* (evil speech) refers only to negative comments made about people behind their backs. In truth, *any* word or gesture which shames another is considered *lashon hara*.

Whether one indulges in *lashon hara* about a person in his presence, or in his absence, or makes statements which, if repeated, would hurt him physically or distress or alarm him — all this is evil *lashon hara*. (Rambam, *Hilchos De'os* 7:5, Ibid., 7:2)

Most people who offend others do so without really meaning to. They should be forgiven quickly, and, if it would be helpful, told of the effect their behavior had on you. Just as a minor cold can be shrugged off easily (by someone whose resistance is strong), so too the pain from this type of unintentional insult can be minimized by telling yourself, "The person did not mean to inflict pain; he was merely unaware or not in control of himself at the moment."

Other people, however, offend deliberately. This behavior constitutes emotional abuse. While it would be immature to take every little offense seriously, it is dangerous and immoral to trivialize or ignore the kind of abuse which is aimed at humiliating, dishonoring and demeaning others. This type of abuse is like a malignancy which will destroy the body if not met with prompt, aggressive treatment.

It is not easy to distinguish the point at which an insensitive remark constitutes abuse. The frequency, intensity and duration of the attacks must be considered. When the attacks are repeated often enough, the results can be disastrous. Many children's lives are turned into nightmares because of the taunting, teasing and bullying of classmates. Teachers make fun of students; parents criticize incessantly. We are even seeing a rise in "elder abuse" by adult children and nursing home attendants. This must be examined with utmost seriousness.

There is no word for the slow destruction of another's spirit. Disrespect kills the spirit, slowly and very painfully. To be constantly scorned by a spouse, sibling, parent, teacher, schoolmate or boss causes terrible psychological damage, leaving the victim feeling worthless and isolated, often for life.

Victims of verbal abuse, especially children, often become convinced that the following damaging beliefs are true:

> "This is what families do — they hound, hurt, humiliate and criticize each other constantly. This is normal behavior."

> "Adults know better, so if I'm rejected and abused, it must be because I'm bad and deserve to be abused. I can do the same to other people who fail to measure up."

> "I'm sure that God hates me too."

In addition to psychological damage, many physical illnesses are directly related to living, working or studying with hostile people. Numerous studies have shown that the immune system is immediately weakened in a hostile atmosphere.

"He who shames another in public has no portion in the World to Come"
• ibid., 6:8 •

Despite this statement, many people ignore the severity of this sin because emotional abuse leaves no immediate physical scars, though the damage can be far greater than that of a beating. Yet many minimize the pain and blithely tell victims, "If you feel hurt, it means you're immature and overly sensitive." Or, "It's just words. Ignore it." This is like telling the victim of a stabbing, "Ignore the pain and the blood." Such attitudes convey the message that hurting people is "no big deal." This attitude actually encourages abuse.

Verbal abuse is a very big deal. Yet the victim, feeling hurt and ashamed, is often revictimized when told, "It's nothing. Forgive and forget." Victims are also hurt by those who jump to the "complicity theory" or "provocationist belief," and tell them, "Somehow you must have deserved it or provoked it." Holding the victim responsible for the criminal's behavior is precisely what allows abuse to flourish because it makes the attacker feel he has done nothing wrong, since he was, after all, "provoked."

Chronic *ona'as devarim* is a major cause of most mental illnesses, including anxiety and depression. Failed relationships, including broken marriages, are almost all due to excessive criticism, a major form of verbal abuse, which is unfortunately all too prevalent in homes and schools. It is often as painful as physical abuse, and the impact can be permanently damaging.

Maintaining the dignity of others is so important that it may even override Halachah at times (*Berachos* 19b). Even when a child or adult needs to be rebuked, his dignity must be preserved (*Sanhedrin* 10a,b).

"THUS GOD SAID TO ISRAEL: 'ALL I ASK IS THAT YOU LOVE
AND RESPECT ONE ANOTHER'"
• TANNA D'VEI ELIYAHU 28 •

"ONE DARE NOT DEMEAN
ANY HUMAN BEING IN THE WORLD"
• ZOHAR VAYETZE 164A •

True, we are taught that one who is forgiving of those who insult him will have all his sins forgiven (*Rosh Hashanah* 17a, Rashi). However, this does not mean that verbal abuse — especially chronic — should be ignored! It is a major transgression and we should all work to eradicate it from our homes, schools and communities — and our own hearts. A person who can walk away from an insulter is at least able to protect himself. But if he lives, works or studies in a hostile atmosphere, his life becomes a nightmare.

WHAT WE SHOULD WE STRIVE FOR

One of the ways by which a person acquires Torah is by displaying the trait of *nosei b'ol im chavero* [to shoulder the emotional burden of others, to feel their pain as if it is one's own] (*Pirkei Avos* 6:6). To be a *nosei b'ol* is the exact opposite of *ona'as devarim*, and is the trait we must cultivate in our homes and schools.

HaRav Yeruchom Levovitz, *zt"l, mashgiach* of Mir Yeshivah in Europe, stated that this trait is even greater than "Love your neighbor as yourself" (*Vayikra* 19:18). In fact, he wrote, "All the mitzvos of the Torah are included in this mitzvah because it is the foundation of the Torah and the mitzvos" (vol. 1, p. 29). *Chazal* characterized *resha'im* (evil people) as those who don't feel another's pain (ibid., p. 31). Lest this frighten the reader, we should be aware that the impulse to condemn exists in all of us. However, if we acknowledge having the impulse and work to restrain it, then we are not truly evil, but rather have moments in which we do evil. Those who are truly evil do not even acknowledge that they have done anything wrong or feel any remorse about having hurt others.

Rabbi Shlomo Wolbe, *shlita,* states that a man's entire spiritual foundation rests on his development as a *nosei b'ol* (*Alei Shur* I, p. 254). In fact, Rabbi Simcha Zissel, the Alter from Kelm, said that the most important criterion for acceptance into his yeshivah was that the student be a *nosei b'ol.* Our task is to become people who are so sensitive to others' feelings that we truly become *nosei b'ol.*

THE URGE TO HURT: A POWERFUL IMPULSE

The impulse to put others down in order to give oneself a sense of superiority and power is a "pleasure" which many people find irresistible. In contrast, a spiritually refined person is always sensitive to the feelings of others. He values every individual and does his utmost not to cause pain.

> "THE LAWS OF *ONA'AS DEVARIM* ARE BASED
> ON THE SUBJECTIVE RESPONSE OF
> THE PERSON YOU ARE TALKING TO"
> • RABBI ZELIG PLISKIN,
> THE POWER OF WORDS,* P. 293 •

> "THE MORE SENSITIVE SOMEONE IS, THE MORE CAREFUL
> YOU MUST BE WHEN TALKING TO HIM"
> • IBID., P. 249 •

Criticism is not "just words."

> "SHAME IS THE GREATEST PAIN"
> • SHABBOS 50B •

We should be as stringent about what comes out of our mouths as we are about what goes in!

* Aish Ha-Torah Publications.

TWO

DEGREES OF
ONA'AS DEVARIM

OVERCOMING THE URGE TO ABUSE

The first step in combating *ona'as devarim* is developing sensitivity to the feelings of others. We can do this by asking others to let us know how they feel about our words and actions. We can listen nondefensively, with compassion, instead of trying to excuse or justify ourselves. We can be aware that each person has his own "touchy" areas. What hurts one may not hurt another. We can decide to never deliberately cause pain to others no matter how justified it may seem at the moment.

We should increase our awareness that each person is created in the Divine image and is, therefore, worthy of respect. We can put this into practice in daily interactions by consciously viewing others — including small children — in this way.

When we feel the urge to shame or humiliate another person, we should get in touch with our motivation by asking ourselves, "Why do I want to make that person feel inadequate or inferior? What am I getting out of this?"

We should realize that denigrating others may cause them to lose their self-esteem. This is not only destructive to them on a personal level, but to society in general. One major result is the breakdown in marriages and other relationships, since people with low self-esteem tend to suffer from depression, anxiety, addictions and other negative behavior.

We can avoid using excuses to abuse others, such as:

"But it's the only way to educate my kids!"

"But these people don't belong to my group, so I don't have to treat them with respect. People who think differently don't deserve respect!"

"But they deserve it!"

"But it's the only way to: get the lazy slob to move/get the insensitive creep to understand me/get the fatso to slim down/get the whining pests to leave me alone!"

"But I'm just being honest."

"But it's impossible to control myself when: I'm in pain/tired/hungry/worried about finances."

"But if I'm insulted, I have to insult back to regain my self-respect. No one gets away with hurting my feelings!"

"But I have to vent my anger or I'll have a heart attack."

"Genetically, our family is prone to being critical."

"I can't change. Being critical is part of my very essence."

"But home is where I have the freedom to say anything!"

"But this is the only vice I have! Everyone needs one vice!"

"But I'm nice most of the time, so that makes up for the times when I explode."

"It doesn't really hurt them. They don't have human feelings."

Recognizing your own "excuse mentality" will help you overcome the urge to abuse.

We can develop tolerance for diversity. The fact that Hashem created no two people alike means that no two people see and feel the same things at all times. Thus, we all sometimes experience a degree of loneliness and frustration with others. When this happens, we have choices: a) we can reject and distance ourselves from them, b) we can hound them with criticism in an attempt to coerce them to be more like ourselves, or c) we can appreciate the fact that God created diversity and respect each person as a unique and Divine individual.

Simply by learning to identify *ona'as devarim* — and encouraging intolerance for verbal abuse — we can reduce its prevalence. And that is the purpose of this book.

DEGREES OF PAIN

To determine whether an offense is *ona'as devarim*, three factors must be taken into consideration: motive, context and tone:

MOTIVE: If the offender had no intention to hurt, he is not guilty of *ona'as devarim*. No one can always be as sensitive as others may desire or always live up to their expectations. There are times when we hurt people unintentionally. This is accidental and not an offense.

CONTEXT: It is also essential to consider the time, the place and the situation. Words which do not hurt at one time may hurt under different circumstances:

ભ *If a family member says, "That looks awful on you," and you know she loves you, and you are still in the store, you might appreciate the comment. Yet the same words might wound deeply if said after you have already purchased the garment.*

ભ *A husband might say in pure innocence, "There isn't enough salt in the soup." However, if he says it in front of guests, and it is the tenth criticism of the day and he speaks in a scornful manner meant to shame his wife and imply that she is incompetent, then this is* ona'as devarim.

TONE: Often, it is not the actual words which cause pain but rather the contempt with which they are said. A person might say, "I'm so happy to see you" with true warmth and joy or icy coldness.

ભ *A person who is prone to hurt others will often cite his "innocent" words to prove that he didn't do anything wrong. The words themselves may not seem harmful to an outsider who is not aware of the tone of voice used at the time or the conditions surrounding the event, but the person who heard them is deeply hurt.*

ASSESSING THE DAMAGE

When speaking about emotional pain, it is important to realize that there are vast differences caused by the frequency, intensity and duration of the hurtful behavior. A family member who rarely makes a sharp remark, and then only under great stress, should be related to differently than a relative who makes daily assaults.

Like burns, the hurt caused by *ona'as devarim* varies in its degree:

FIRST DEGREE — ACCIDENTAL: At this level, there is no intention to hurt you. The person might have made a remark about your dress or way of life, not realizing that you would be hurt by the comment. The person you phone sometimes may hurt you by being too busy to speak, or giving you a trite answer when you mention a personal loss or make a statement which triggers a wound they know nothing about.

For example, asking a person, "What does your husband do?" is usually not hurtful, unless that person is a widow or divorcee. We cannot be blamed if there was no way of knowing beforehand that the person thus spoken to was sensitive in that area. (It's a good idea not to ask such a question if we have no way of knowing whether or not it will be hurtful.) However, once we know that a person is sensitive, then repeating offensive remarks on sensitive subjects makes us guilty of *ona'as devarim*.

Hurt which is truly unintentional is not *ona'as devarim*. For example:

ଔ *Pressed for time, X does not return Y's phone call until two days later.*

- ✿ X forgets Y's birthday or anniversary.

- ✿ X visits Y at a time inconvenient to Y.

- ✿ X forgets to invite Y to his simchah or invites him but fails to give him the honor he expected.

- ✿ Due to other engagements, X doesn't attend Y's simchah.

- ✿ Being disorganized, X unintentionally leaves a mess which bothers Y, who is very meticulous and fastidious.

- ✿ X speaks proudly about how well his children are doing in school, not realizing that Y, whose children have learning disabilities, feels hurt.

People can also offend unintentionally, mistakenly thinking they are doing you a favor. For example:

- ✿ X gives Y advice which causes a loss to Y, as in an unwise financial investment or improper medical treatment.

- ✿ X gives Y a gift which Y feels must be displayed, even though Y dislikes the item.

- ✿ X fixes up two single people who are totally inappropriate for each other.

- ✿ Teacher X tells parent Y how poorly her child is doing, thinking the parent will now get help for him, not knowing that Y feels so discouraged that she goes home and hits the child, berates him constantly for being stupid or ignores him from then on.

People differ greatly in the degree of self-disclosure with which they are comfortable. Some people feel hurt if you do not show interest by asking personal questions. Others are offended when asked the same questions.

If you feel hurt, the knowledge that your pain was caused accidentally will lessen its sting considerably.

SECOND DEGREE — OFFENSIVE BUT NOT ABUSIVE: People at this level are annoying, not to be malicious, but because of lack of awareness, bad manners, lack of self-control or an underdeveloped conscience. Just as each person has an IQ, so does each person have an EQ (Emotional Quotient). People can cause pain with their low EQ because they are not concerned with others' feelings and can be very irresponsible and insensitive.

For example:

- *X never calls his wife to say he will be late, doesn't express thanks for the meal she cooked and turns on the news while she is talking.*

- *X doesn't return things he borrowed or returns them in a damaged condition and does not offer to pay for them.*

- *X clears the dishes in the middle of her husband's d'var Torah, forgets to mail his letters and often misplaces his important papers.*

- *X eats noisily or with an open mouth, leaves a mess around or makes noise when others are sleeping.*

- *X says, "I could have gotten it for you cheaper" after Y already bought an item and cannot return it.*

Others are critical because:

It makes them feel powerful especially during moments of pain, helplessness, or frustration, or

they think it is the only way to change you, to educate you, to get you to respond to their needs or see things from their point of view, or

they think that their ability to point out your faults proves that they are perceptive and intelligent, or

they feel hurt by you and want to hurt you back, or

they think you are so incompetent that you must be constantly criticized to save you from disaster, not realizing that this only makes you feel even more stupid and inept, or

they need to maintain a sense of distance, because closeness feels dangerous to them, or

they crave closeness and think closeness means sameness; so they try to coerce you into being a copy of their own image with constant criticism, or

they are insecure and think they will feel safe only by acting obnoxiously and then seeing if you'll forgive them.

Communicating with people like this is tricky. Often, if you say you feel hurt, the person becomes even more defensive and hostile. You need to employ great sensitivity and numerous tactics to get your point across. And even then, you still might not succeed.

THIRD DEGREE — CONSCIOUS CRUELTY: When people use words or facial expressions to control, belittle and terrorize others, this is *ona'as devarim* at its worst. Like a third-degree burn, the hurt caused by this type of verbal abuse penetrates deeply and often leaves victims with a permanent sense of worthlessness.

People who purposely dominate and belittle, and do so compulsively, are like alcoholics. They suffer from a serious and dangerous addiction called Abusive Personality Disorder (APD).

To gain total control over others, those with APD use a range of cruel tactics such as violent explosions and cruel coldness, alternating with moments of charm and friendliness. Those with APD have no sense of guilt or remorse for the pain they cause others nor sympathy for their victims. If they do apologize, it is only to win back the person's trust, and once that is accomplished, they begin attacking again. Their compulsion to undermine and humiliate is as compelling as any addictive craving.

Many people with APD are very charming to those whom they want to influence, while terrorizing others. Or they are alternately charming and cruel, or nasty only to one family member while nice to others. This double personality phenomenon makes the victims thoroughly confused and constantly agitated.

People with APD almost never go to therapy since they do not recognize that they have a problem. They think they are reacting to provocations in a justified manner and that their moments of niceness make up for whatever they do the rest of the time.

What is very confusing about people with APD is that their public image is often so very different from their private behavior. They are often in positions of power and may be dynamic community activists, generous philanthropists and seemingly friendly, normal human beings. Outsiders would never imagine the viciousness which erupts only in the privacy of their own homes.

Advisors will implore the victim to "just give in" or "communicate" to enhance the relationship. They do not realize that communicating with a person with APD is usually futile, since they become incredibly unreasonable and irrational when you try to get a point across. You suddenly feel as though you have walked straight into a wall or, to be more accurate, into a whirling propeller. Any attempt to explain your side of the story is met with justifications, ridicule, denial, lies, threats and counter-accusations, such as, "How dare you talk to me like this!"/"I never hurt you."/ "There you go again, getting all emotional. You're crazy."/ "I'm just trying to help you improve."/"I'm the real victim."/ "I'm just standing up for my rights."

It's not so much the hostile words which affect their victims as it is the poisonous message underlying the words, i.e., "You're crazy, defective, stupid and worthless." The words may only last a few seconds, but the hostile message may be internalized forever.

Like the nuclear explosion in Chernobyl, no normal person can avoid being affected by the hostility which is radiated during an attack of *ona'as devarim*. Even if the victim of the attack walks away silently as if nothing has happened, his heart has been wounded.

Outsiders usually tell victims that they should just try harder to please the one who is attacking them and blame the one who complains for failing to meet their impossible standards or for not being able to remain calm and indifferent in the face of their punitive rages. Advisors often implore the victim to keep trying to please the abuser.

But people with APD are "unpleasable." Thus, for example, a mother with APD might tell her daughter to bring her a glass of water, then berate her for not bringing it faster, for using the wrong glass, for not having thought to bring the water without her having to ask, for leaving a water ring on the table, for not coming back to fetch the glass immediately or for not washing it properly. And this may be only one of hundreds of such interactions a day! The mother complains to others that her daughter is distant or insolent, never thinking that she has contributed to the problem in any way.

Similarly, a wife should definitely do everything in her power to make her husband happy, but what if he tells her that she must not kiss her babies because that will spoil them or insists that she adopt religious stringencies which cause her great pain? Any advisor who encourages her to please him is giving her false hopes, since this is impossible.

Like many people with severe addictions, people with APD often seem quite normal to outsiders. Few realize how devastating this emotional illness is to the victims. The Blame-the-Victim syndrome is so common that little if any outside pressure is ever brought against those who do the most damage.

THREE

How to Recognize an Offender and an Offense

WHO ABUSES?

Emotional illness is manifested in many different ways. It is a common error to assume that all disturbed people feel profoundly insecure and inferior. In fact, of those most likely to engage in abusive behavior, some actually suffer from an attitude of superiority and grandiosity. Only possessive phobics, the last of those mentioned below, may seem quite pitiful and more obviously neurotic. Yet all of them tend to be extremely critical of the way others behave and enjoy restricting and punishing, heaping scorn on those who cannot meet their demands or keep their oppressive rules and regulations:

HARSH MORALISTS: These unaffectionate, austere, overly strict types think it is their duty to force their morality on the rest of humanity. Obsessed with details, cleanliness, order and rigid rules, they often adopt excessively harsh religious standards and look down on all those who do not meet their standards, considering them evil.

STUNNING SUPERSTARS: These coldly competitive types are extremely jealous and status conscious. They feel compelled to outshine everyone. They and their family members must be the smartest, richest, most famous, most elegant and most successful of all.

OPPRESSIVE DICTATORS: Brutal and often physically violent, these types relate to people as masters to slaves. Others are likely to feel totally insignificant and invisible in their presence.

POSSESSIVE PHOBICS: Unlike the others, they are plagued by anxiety, insecurity and fears of abandonment. Extremely possessive and jealous, they put others down to assuage their own feelings of inferiority. They see themselves as pathetic and in the victim role. They may also have obsessive-compulsive disorders and tend to be unstable and unpredictable. Their fearful imagination makes them highly anxious. Extremely suspicious, they are convinced that others will betray them. Thus they feel they have the right to limit others' freedom of thought and movement.

These types of people have serious emotional disturbances. Do not blame yourself for their behavior, for then you will not be able to protect yourself in the assertive manner which is required. Remember, you can never please them, at least not for long. In their distorted minds, they must see you in a negative light in order to justify their cruelty. Thus, a parent will often call a child "bad boy/girl" before administering a beating. By viewing the child as bad, they then feel justified in hurting the child. This same attitude prevails in their relationships with others.

ATTACHMENT DISORDERS:
WHY THEY LEAD TO ABUSE

There are many reasons why a person becomes abusive. The main one is due to the lack of a strong, secure bond of love between the person as a young child and his parents. If a parent dies or the child is neglected, abandoned, abused or lives in an anxiety-ridden atmosphere, he cannot form an attachment of secure love with his parents.

Those with attachment disorders don't believe that anyone's love can be permanent, including God's love. Family bonds, which should be as strong as steel, seem transitory and as unreliable as a spider's web, since their only experience with love is that it is here one minute and gone the next.

Because people have proven so untrustworthy, those with attachment disorders constantly fear being "burned," — i.e., rejected, criticized or abandoned. Their relationships tend to be frought with anxiety and conflict. The "loving disabled" are easily offended, concluding all too quickly that no one really cares about them. Some withdraw to protect themselves from the pain of being either the rejecter or the rejectee. Some try to force those closest to them to satisfy whatever physical and emotional needs were neglected early in their lives, not realizing that this may feel stifling or abusive to others.

Those who have not experienced trust in relationships have difficulty loving generously and unconditionally. They live with a profound sense of inner lonliness which no activity or person can relieve for long. Thus, it seems only logical to become:

> ল Excessively fragile, clingy, needy, helpless and dependent.

> ল Excessively suspicious, questioning and possessive.

> ল Excessively punitive, domineering and cruel.

os Excessively cold, withdrawn, aloof.

Thankfully, it is possible to recover from such disorders by learning to respect and value oneself and others unconditionally, in keeping with the laws of Torah.

ARE YOU JUDGING CORRECTLY?

Although abusive behavior is common, it is very important not to judge other people as deliberately offensive unless you know the situation very well over a long period of time.

This is especially true for those who grew up with physical or verbal abuse. In such cases, they may be too quick to judge unintentional slights (First Degree — p.26) as deliberate attacks (Third Degree — p.30). Having been insulted and rejected as children, they tend to perceive ordinary people as being hostile and attacking them deliberately. Every time a person is late, unsympathetic, unavailable, fails to return a phone call or fails to respond to their needs, they may perceive it as intentional, and attack back or withdraw in bitter resentment.

We are all required to judge average people favorably (*Avos* 1:6). But those who were often hurt in the past must be especially careful to assume that most offenses are First or Second Degree (unless, of course, the person is a habitual offender). They can then forgive or speak about their feelings in a compassionate, nonaccusatory manner.

This will be difficult at first, especially since even the most minor snub can trigger all the pain of past hurts. However, as one practices classifying hurts as First or Second Degree, trust in most people's basic goodness will take hold in one's consciousness.

Good communication is like fine-tuning an instrument. Even the most skilled person may not always "get it right" and can accidentally offend, due to his own pain or pre-occupations. Therefore, we should all make constant, conscious efforts to be compassionate, to avoid taking minor slights personally and to constantly look for the positive in people.

On the other hand, those who have suffered severe hurt in the past may be acutely sensitive to true hostility, both hidden and overt, correctly perceiving it more quickly than less sensitized types. They will be frustrated when others deny what is so obvious to them.

THE JEWISH WAY

Almost everyone is guilty of being insensitive at times, albeit inadvertently. We can only strive not to be this way intentionally.

Our Sages tell us, "If something disgraceful happened to someone's relative, do not say anything in his presence that will remind him of it. For example, if someone's relative was hanged, do not mention the term hanging in his presence, even in the context of hanging [a picture] on the wall." (Bava Metzia 59a; Orach Meisharim 5:3 — quoted from Rabbi Zelig Pliskin, Love Your Neighbor,[*] p. 294)

---

[*] Aish Ha-Torah Publications.

"WHEN A MAN SINS AGAINST ANOTHER,
THE INJURED PARTY SHOULD NOT HATE THE OFFENDER
AND NOT KEEP SILENT, BUT IT IS HIS DUTY
TO INFORM THE OFFENDER.
IF THE OFFENDER ASKS FOR FORGIVENESS,
HE SHOULD BE FORGIVEN.
HOWEVER, IF ONE IS WRONGED AND DOES NOT WISH TO
REBUKE OR SPEAK TO THE OFFENDER BECAUSE THE
LATTER IS A SIMPLETON OR MENTALLY CONFUSED,
AND INSTEAD SINCERELY FORGIVES HIM,
BEARING HIM NO ILL-WILL, AND DOES NOT REBUKE HIM,
THEN THIS IS CONSIDERED *MIDDAS CHASSIDUS*,
EXEMPLARY BEHAVIOR"
• HILCHOS DE'OS 6:6 AND 6:9 •

Some people feel that they have a right to say whatever they wish and that it is up to those who have to hear them to work on themselves not to be hurt by what they hear.

"It's not what I say to you that causes you pain," they will say. "Rather, it's the way that you take it. It's your own attitude that is causing you the suffering. Change your attitude and you won't have any problem. Since it's all your fault, I don't need to be careful with what I say to you." Yes, it is true that a person's subjective evaluation of a statement is what causes him emotional pain. But this does not give anyone the right to insult others and claim that they should develop coping skills.

"IF A PERSON DOES FEEL PAIN, YOU ARE FORBIDDEN TO
SAY ANYTHING THAT WILL CAUSE HIM THAT PAIN"
• RABBI ZELIG PLISKIN,
THE POWER OF WORDS,* P. 158 •

---

* Aish Ha-Torah Publications.

REMEMBER THAT THIS HOLDS TRUE
FOR CHILDREN TOO!

If you are constantly offended and cannot express your pain to the offender, the relationship will eventually die, for healthy relationships are built on honest communication. If, when you tell a person that a remark hurt you, he attacks you for complaining, you have hit against a stone wall and will probably require outside help. If a less abusive type says, "You're just touchy," you might let him know, "Yes, I am very sensitive to this sin." Remind him that when Sarah told Avraham that Hagar was humiliating her, Avraham did not say, "Don't take it seriously; you're too touchy." God told him to listen to Sarah and he banished Hagar (*Bereshis* 21:9-12).

Verbal abuse is real and it is deadly. It can destroy the will to live and the ability to love and feel loved.

FOUR

FIFTY CAUSES OF
EMOTIONAL PAIN

There are many ways words can be used as weapons. Some examples are listed below. In some instances, POSSIBLE SOLUTIONS (indicated by the ☞ sign) are provided. However, do not assume that these solutions will always work! Change is difficult for all of us. If you are dealing with people who have APD (Abusive Personality Disorder — where the person engages in emotional cruelty, but takes no responsibility for his actions, claiming unawareness concerning the effect of his behavior on others), remember that they think they are fine and that *you* are the problem! Calling attention to any imperfection is likely to arouse a furious defense.

Also, if you yourself have been very critical of others in the past, they may not trust your new-found efforts to be nicer. If you have built a "Great Wall of China" between you and the person with your critical remarks, it will take a long time for them to trust that you are no longer a threat. As with any addiction, it takes years of persistent efforts to build trust.

The following list contains many types of emotional pain, some of which do not fall into the strict category of *ona'as devarim*, but rather are Torah prohibitions against gossip, indifference, hatred, shaming, vengeance or grudge-bearing. Others are in the category of insensitivity or bad manners. Whether or not one takes the broad view of the

Pele Yo'etz (op cit.), that any deliberate act which hurts another's feelings is *ona'as devarim*, the important thing is to become more aware. This will make you more careful.

Do not attack those who fail to heed the prohibition against hurting others' feelings. Rather, try to simply sensitize them about this matter. When you yourself fail, apologize quickly and promise yourself to be more careful next time.

1. ACCUSING OTHERS OF PURPOSELY TRYING TO HURT YOU, EVEN IF THEY HAD NO INTENTION OF DOING SO: In the course of the day, things get lost, broken, worn out and damaged. People are sometimes forgetful, insensitive or not always on the ball. An emotionally healthy person says, "That's life — mistakes can happen. People are imperfect." He either ignores these petty losses or finds a solution. But a disturbed person accuses others of doing these things *davka* [purposely], creating a tense atmosphere of mistrust.

TO SPOUSE:
"You purposely didn't get my things from the cleaners! You don't care a hoot about me."

"You purposely kept me waiting so I'd miss my appointment."

"Where did you hide my glasses?" (Note the accusation implied in the word "hide.")

"That's the third time you've told me to pay the bill. You think I'm an untrustworthy idiot!"

"Take out the garbage? You want to turn me into your slave!"

"What's this bill? You're trying to destroy me!

You just married me for my money!"

"Crying again? You're just trying to manipulate me!"

PARENT TO CHILD:
"You *davka* have to go to the bathroom every time I get to the check-out counter!"

"You stole my money."

"You are really trying to drive me crazy, aren't you!"

"You left a mess on purpose for me to clean up!"

"You didn't do your homework just so I'd scream!"

"You're moving slowly just to make me crazy."

"You spilled your juice on purpose, you little brat!"

"You left that box on the step so I'd fall and break my neck!"

"You have to talk to me *just* when I get on the phone!"

CHILD TO PARENT:
"You hate me. That's why you asked me to do this chore! You want to turn me into your slave."

"You *davka* won't buy me what I want! You're so mean."

"You *davka* made fish tonight even though you know I hate it!"

☞ **FOR ACCUSERS:**

Even if, based on past experience, you think there is a speck of truth in what you are saying, such hostile accusations and judgments are still destructive and self-defeating. Mind-reading is especially hurtful, as in:

"I know why you are being nice. You just want something from me."

☞ **FOR MIND-READERS:**

It is offensive to others when you assume that you know what is in another person's heart or head and to assume that they have ulterior motives, unless long experience with the person has proven you correct.

In most cases, assume that the person did not mean to hurt you on purpose. Often, their actions may have nothing to do with you. Perhaps they simply forgot, were careless, exercised poor judgment, were in pain or weren't even thinking about you at the moment. Don't jump to hostile conclusions. Instead, ask for information:

"Did you do that on purpose, or am I just being paranoid?"

"I was so worried when you didn't come on time. You are usually so responsible. What happened?"

State your feelings with an "I" message:

"I feel hurt. Can we talk about it?"

"I am missing money. Do you know where it might be?"

"We have to make some rules so that this does not happen again."

"Everyone makes mistakes. That was a learning experience."

☞ **FOR VICTIMS:**
Unless the person accusing you is paranoid, calmly explain your side. However, if the person has an emotional disturbance, he is probably convinced that you have hurt him deliberately. Any excuse you give will be used as ammunition to attack you. The more you protest and say, "But I do love you/trust you," the more fiercely they argue to prove their point, bringing even more evidence to prove that you really are as bad as they say you are. Eventually, you'll get furious about their accusations and then they will have the evidence they have sought! This is very painful. Try to keep distant from such people. Do not blame yourself for their behavior.

2. ARGUING OVER PETTY ISSUES FOR NO OTHER REASON EXCEPT TO ARGUE: Most people who nitpick have a lust to be right and use any issue, no matter how petty. They will argue about turning on the fan in the summer and the heat in winter, about every purchase and every request.

If one person asks for something, the other will reply, "But you don't really need it. You can get along without it." For example, when a spouse says, "Please take out the garbage," the other will consistently reply, "But it's not full enough yet."

ભ *"I asked my son to bring me twenty chairs from a neighbor for a simchah I'm having. He replied, "But you only need fifteen." If I had asked for fifteen, he would have said I should get ten or perhaps twenty. He just has to have the upper hand."*

CHILD TO PARENT:

"I won't do the dishes! It's her turn! You're always picking on me."

"I won't wear these hand-me-downs."

"But I took a bath last week!"

☞ FOR ARGUERS:

Become aware of your tendency to argue. Catch yourself five times a day when you are about to disagree. At these times, try letting go of your need to be right and to prove everyone else wrong.

☞ FOR VICTIMS:

Be firm, not hostile. Calmly repeat the request like a broken record. Practice in front of a mirror to get the right tone of voice — authoritative but non-condemnatory. Say: "I will tell you when a request is negotiable. This is not negotiable. I will not discuss this any further." When an argumentative child does not argue, point it out. Hug him and tell him how much you appreciate his cooperation.

Note: Some people suffer from ODD (Oppositional Defiance Disorder) and need psychiatric help. However, expect that the person will oppose your attempts to get him to see a therapist!

3. BAITING DELIBERATELY: This means provoking someone with insulting, irritating remarks, as in:

TO SPOUSE:

"I know you hate me/don't really care/don't trust me."

RELATIVE TO RELATIVE:

"Why don't you visit more often?"

"Is that what you call a meal?"

CHILD TO CHILD:
"How come you wear those clothes?"

"How come you flunked?"

"How come you talk like that?"

NOSY NEIGHBOR:
"You make your husband do the shopping?"

"You let your children go on the bus alone?"

"Aren't you being too strict/lenient with your children?"

MOTHER-IN-LAW TO DAUGHTER-IN-LAW:
"My son hasn't looked well since he married you. Didn't your mother teach you to cook?"

"Didn't you ever learn how to clean a house?"

"So few children and you need a maid?"

"He still isn't toilet trained?"

TO A PERSON WHO HOLDS DIFFERENT RELIGIOUS VIEWS:
"Aren't you going overboard? You don't have to be so strict, you know. You think you're holier than everyone else?"

"If you were really religious, you wouldn't wear makeup."

☞ **FOR BAITERS:**

Don't look for reasons to put others down. If you are feeling hostile or superior, don't say anything.

☞ **FOR VICTIMS:**

Use the "fogging technique." Instead of arguing, say: "You have a point."/"What you say makes sense."/"You're right. I do have a lot of faults."/"True. Cooking isn't my strong point."/"You're right. I am sensitive. I do cry easily."

4. BETRAYING CONFIDENCES: Telling over information which someone confided in you is a betrayal of that person's trust. For example:

> ෫ Telling one person that another person doesn't like him.

> ෫ Telling someone that a relative is taking medication for an emotional problem.

> ෫ Talking about a child's problem to another person (especially when the child is present!), such as the fact that he is a bed-wetter, a slob, or a poor student.

> ෫ Telling someone that a family has a genetic disorder (unless a *shidduch* is involved).

5. BLAMING PEOPLE FOR THEIR PERSONAL TRAGEDIES: We are told, "Do not be like the 'friends' of Job who told him that he was to blame for his illness and suffering" (*Bava Metzia* 58). Thus, we should not tell people:

> "It's your own stupidity which brought this about."

> "God's punishing you."

True, when suffering comes to a person, he should examine his deeds, but not in a way which makes him feel hated or abandoned by God. If appropriate at some later time, one might suggest, in a gentle manner, "Perhaps you can examine your past behavior or take upon yourself to be extra careful about a particular mitzvah in order to give your suffering meaning."

Rabbi Yaakov Yisrael Baifus brings down ten different reasons as to why we suffer, according to our Sages. Only one of these is punishment. No one knows which of the ten is applicable to any given person. (*Longing for Dawn*, translated by Rabbi Nachman Bulman, pp. 87-105.)

Likewise, it is very common for victims of abuse to be told:

> "You are being abused? It's only because you are not trying hard enough to please."

> "You must have provoked him/her."

> "It's because you don't know how to communicate and because you're too _____ (demanding, passive, smart, talkative, disorganized, sensitive, nervous, etc.)."

People like to think that abuse is always the result of something the victim did. By blaming the one who suffers, this makes the world seem "fair" and the suffering justified. The truth is that a disturbed person always finds an excuse to pick on others in order to justify his nastiness.

Another destructive form of blame is to try to make people feel responsible for your general unhappiness and personal mistakes, as when one family member tells another,

> "It's all your fault that I never amounted to any-

thing and that I've had nothing but misery all my life!"

6. BOASTING: Sharing positive experiences with others can enhance relationships. But going overboard about one's talents and successes, especially to those who cannot accomplish the same, can hurt others. It is commonly thought that boasters feel secretly inferior. In truth, however, many boasters actually feel quite superior. Instead of recognizing that their talents and accomplishments are gifts from God, they feel that they are specially favored and that they have rights and privileges which those "lower" than themselves do not deserve. They cannot resist the urge to let others know:

> NEIGHBOR TO NEIGHBOR:
> "All my children are the best in their classes!"
>
> "My children jump when I snap my fingers. It would never even occur to them not to cooperate!"
>
> "I get along with everyone. What's wrong with you that you can't?"
>
> "I finished all my Pesach cleaning two weeks before Pesach."
>
> "I manage just fine on four hours of sleep."
>
> "I stay calm no matter what's going on."
>
> "I'm back at work a week after I give birth."
>
> "I have twice as many grandchildren and I'm younger!"

CHILD TO CHILD:
"Your father works and mine studies, so my father is better than your father."

One-upping is a form of boasting. No matter what someone says, this person says he can do it better.

"It took you five minutes? I could have done it in three."

"He was toilet trained at three? Mine was trained at two."

"You paid how much? I got it for half that price."

☞ FOR VICTIMS:
Refuse to engage in neurotic interchanges. Change the game by diverting the attention of one-uppers. Don't ever let someone else's boast make you feel inferior. Realize that it's nothing but their desperate attempt to feel important. The best response is often a polite, "That's very nice," accompanied by the secure thought that it is Hashem who gives people their talents and strengths. Hashem gives you value, not other people.

7. BRINGING UP PAINFUL EVENTS FROM THE PAST: In *Bava Metzia* (58b), we are told not to remind people of past mistakes if doing so would cause them pain, such as:

"Before you were *frum*, you used to..."

"You're screaming again, just like when you had your nervous breakdown and went into a major depression."

☞ FOR REMINDERS:
Let go of the past. Everyone has the right to make a fresh

start. Seek to uplift others and give them hope.

☞ **FOR VICTIMS:**
Give yourself messages of hope. "I deserve love for who I am right now. The fact that I am alive proves that God loves me and wants me in the world."

8. COMPARING OTHERS IN A WAY WHICH MAKES THEM FEEL INFERIOR: Comparing family members to others who are inside or outside the family only makes the family members feel they are unaccepted for who they are. It also creates animosity between those being compared.

SPOUSE TO SPOUSE:
"There you go again, acting just like your mother/father!" (Said with full awareness that the person has a terrible relationship with that relative.)

"My parent/sibling would never do that!"

HUSBAND TO WIFE:
"My mother is a better cook than you are and she's so much more efficient — she cleans up in half the time."

"My sister sews her own clothes, has a child every year, holds a full-time job, is always smiling, keeps her house looking like a museum and never asks her husband for help."

WIFE TO HUSBAND:
"My brother is so much more successful than you are."

CHILD TO MOTHER:
"The other mothers make fancy cakes with all

kinds of decorations."

"All my friends' mothers are having babies."

"Why don't you go to an exercise class so you can look like Mrs. Y?"

PARENT TO CHILD:
"Why can't you be good/thin/smart like your older sister?"

"Your cousins are so much more spiritual!"

"Mrs. G's children behave so much better than you! They never argue and they always help."

CHILD TO CHILD:
"What's taking you so long? I could do those math problems in a second."

TEACHER TO STUDENT:
"Too bad you're not as smart as your older brother."

NEIGHBOR TO NEIGHBOR:
"You pamper yourself with three days in the hospital after giving birth? I'm home within twenty-four hours and start cooking and cleaning straightaway!"

☞ FOR COMPARERS:
Appreciate the fascinating variety of people in the world. Value each person just as God values each person. To develop a "good eye," give two compliments a day to the person you tend to have most difficulty accepting. If you're looking for the positive, you will find it. Be a person who looks for the good; it's a sign of spiritual greatness.

9. COMPLAINING/SULKING ON A CONSTANT BASIS: Everyone has bad moods at times, but chronic complainers pull others into a negative whirlpool of gloom with their endless complaints about everyone and everything.

TO SPOUSE:
"The rice is stuck together."/"The weather is so crummy."/"The napkins don't match the tablecloth."/"There's dust on the picture tops."/"My shirts aren't white enough."/"Everything here is a mess."

CHILD TO PARENT:
"You never take me anywhere."/"You never buy me anything."/"You always take his/her side."

PARENT TO CHILD:
"You're lisping again. Be quiet! Stop sucking your thumb. Your room is a mess. Stop being so spacey."

NEIGHBOR TO NEIGHBOR:
"Oy, let me tell you about my problems. I have pain from my head to my toes. Every part of me hurts."/"I have it worse than anyone. I don't get enough (love, attention, money, etc.)."/"My children are so ungrateful and so messed up."/"I always get ripped off."/"I can't trust anyone."/"Oy, the people in this community are so phony and cold."/"Life is so unfair."/"Nobody understands me."

☞ FOR PARENTS:
Learn to use positive reinforcement instead.

☞ FOR COMPLAINERS:
You are suffering from a "bad eye" syndrome (see *Pirkei*

Avos 2:10). This is a malady which can be healed with self-discipline. You might *kvetch* less if you:

ଔ Read *Tehillim* each day. Strengthen your *emunah* and *bitachon* by internalizing the truth that God gives you exactly what you need for your mission in life.

ଔ Keep a "Gratefulness Notebook" in which you write down ten things a day for which you are grateful.

ଔ Say something positive to someone every hour on the hour. If no one is around, thank Hashem for something.

ଔ Learn to listen. Don't have a one-sided grumble; let others share their pain with you.

ଔ Smile, even if it is insincere. It is good for your immune system. Remember, we are told, "Greet every man with a cheerful countenance" (*Pirkei Avos* 1:15). A forced act of positive behavior improves the mood (*Sefer Ha-chinuch* #16).

ଔ Be aware of when you are having a "pity party." Write down your negative thoughts, then write counter-balancing positive ones.

ଔ Get active! Contribute something positive to the world instead of dwelling on your own pain. Giving to others is the best way to feel better.

Be patient with yourself, for it takes time to change negative thinking patterns. It is very similar to giving up cigarettes.

☞ **FOR VICTIMS:**

People feel better when they share their pain. However, chronic grumblers become more depressed the more they grumble. They can break this habit only by learning to value and to be enthusiastic about what is positive in life. Encourage them to write down the smallest blessings. Share your own Gratefulness Notebook with them. Children who *kvetch* a lot can be given a small coin for each item they write down in their own Gratefulness Notebook. Or, say, "I take you seriously. Let's list each of your complaints and find a solution to each one." Some grumblers do not want solutions; complaining is the only way they know of "engaging" with people and they don't know other alternatives.

10. CRIMINALIZING INNOCENT BEHAVIOR: It is wrong to make another person feel like a criminal, especially when he has committed no sin. If it's not mentioned in the *Shulchan Aruch* as a sin, it's not a sin! However, hurting people with words is a sin, as in:

> TO SPOUSE:
> "Idiot. How could you pay so much for this garbage?"
>
> "Jerk! Look at how dirty this is!"
>
> "Lost your keys? You are a total idiot!"
>
> "Incompetent! You didn't put the cap back on the jar! You left coffee stains in the sink! There's dust on the shelves!"

Children are often made to feel like criminals for non-sins:

> PARENT TO CHILD:
> "Dummy! You got less than 100% on the test!"

"Selfish! You finished all the ketchup in the house!"

"Naughty boy! You didn't finish your meal!"

"Clumsy idiot! You spilled your juice!"

"There you go, trying to get my attention again, you brat!"

"Bad girl! You wet your bed again!"

☞ **FOR CRIMINALIZERS:**
Do the following:

> ೞ Your foremost commandment is to love God (*Devarim* 6:4). You express love for God by loving your fellowman.

> ೞ Whatever you consider a sin is not as bad as the sin of shaming others, which is akin to murder.

> ೞ The urge to demonize people is wrong. Don't justify it!

> ೞ To help reconstruct your distorted value system, draw a 10 cm. ruler. Designate "10" as a major sin. Decide that from right now, anything below "5" will be considered a triviality or a mere annoyance. Be aware of when you are turning a "1" into a "10." Focus calmly on solutions.

☞ **FOR VICTIMS:**
Some people enjoy playing a perverse game called "Uproar," the object of which is to make mountains out of molehills, thereby keeping the attention focused on them-

selves and keeping everyone in the household tense, if not terrified. Explain the ruler trick to them — if they'll listen! If they refuse to listen, you must withdraw and disconnect to whatever degree possible under such adverse conditions.

11. CRITICIZING: An occasional critical remark about a person's present behavior may hurt, but will usually not cause much damage if the relationship is basically positive. What is especially harmful is when one person makes a global indictment of another person's very essence and does so constantly and obsessively.

> TO SPOUSE:
> "You're selfish, stupid and lazy and you can't do anything right."
>
> "You're a total disappointment to me."
>
> "You always make the dumbest decisions."
>
> PARENT TO CHILD:
> "You're a lazy slob and a spoiled brat. Plus, you never listen. And you never cooperate and you always make a mess. You just can't do anything right."

Double binding is an insidious form of criticism in which anything you do to please others is seen as wrong.

> ෴ If you talk, they attack whatever you say; but if you are silent, they attack you for being withdrawn and secretive.

> ෴ They tell you to visit more often; but when you do, they complain about what a burden you are.

⍥ They say you're wasting your life by being a housewife; but if you go out to work, they accuse you of neglecting the children.

⍥ They complain that you are pampering the children; but when you discipline the kids, they say you're cruel.

☞ **FOR CRITICIZERS:**
Constantly telling people that they are crazy, stupid, selfish or total failures does nothing but put them into despair. One who invalidates others, does so because of his own shortcomings (*Kiddushin* 70a). Rebuke is not criticism. Rebuke is a mitzvah (*Vayikra* 19:17) which is done out of love, to help elevate the other person.

☞ **FOR VICTIMS OF OCCASIONAL CRITICISM:**
Though *ona'as devarim* is never justified, prepare yourself ahead of time to respond to non-abusive comments calmly by considering:

⍥ Is there is a speck of truth to the comment? If so, let them know you are trying to improve! For example, if you are messy, say, "See, I put my dirty clothes in the hamper!" If you are often late, say, "See, I'm right on time." [*Note*: People with APD can never be pleased. No matter how hard you try, they retain their negative view of you to justify their cruelty. Do not try to convince yourself that their intentions are honorable!]

⍥ Maybe the person does not want to hurt you? Maybe he simply lacks sensitivity about this matter? Maybe he is in pain and does not realize what he is saying? If the person spoke in a scornful tone, calmly ask him to repeat the request in a respectful voice. If the person is emotionally healthy, this will help him realize that you have been hurt, yet that you care about the message he needs to get across.

○ Maybe the person wants to feel closer to you? If so, make some gesture which will make the person feel cared for, such as discussing subjects that interest the person, even if they are not of such great interest to you.

○ Can I defuse the situation by agreeing? For example:

"You have a point. Tell me specifically how you would like me to improve."

"It's true. I do tend to be _____."

"You have a point. I am quite shy. I can change the way Hashem made me." (See my books *Appreciating People** and *Awareness** for insight into innate nature vs. *middos*.)

○ Do I have to respond? The compulsion to respond traps many people into neurotic interactions. Be proud of your self-control. Remember that "The whole world exists only in the merit of he who bridles his mouth during a quarrel" (*Chullin* 89a). Thinking that you're helping to keep the world in existence by your silence is something positive to focus on at such painful times. You might also pray for them, that they should have a *refuah shelemah* from their mental disturbance.

* Feldheim Publishers.

However, do not deny the pain of being around a person who is chronically hostile. Many advisors tell the spouse to pay no attention to critical remarks. And many spouses pride themselves on being able to act as if they are not bothered by them. But this is a charade. The truth is that chronic criticism is devastating both physically and emotionally. After twenty or thirty years, the victim suddenly breaks and cannot bear it anymore. This is because the expression of animosity leads to greater animosity; criticizers become more hostile the more they criticize. And the damage to the victim is cumulative. When the breaking point comes, there may be no turning back.

12. CURSING: There is a specific Torah prohibition against cursing (*Vayikra* 19:14). However, people without spiritual refinement ignore the "duties of the heart," such as compromise, forgiveness and compassion. They prefer tactics such as cursing to provide themselves with an illusion of having God-like power over others. This prohibition does not apply when mentioning the names of publically acknowledged enemies of the Jewish people.

CHILD TO PARENT:
"I wish you were dead."

PARENT TO CHILD:
"I hope your children do the same thing to you."

"You'll never get married! Nobody will ever want to marry you."

There is no place for cursing another Jew at any time, under any circumstances.

13. DEMANDING PERFECTION: Demanding perfection from others is a cruel form of emotional abuse.

TO SPOUSE:
"I love you only when you live up to all my expectations."

HUSBAND TO WIFE:
"I don't care if you have three kids in diapers. I want the house perfectly clean at all times and don't ever let the kids make noise!"

WIFE TO HUSBAND:
"If you really loved me, you'd stay up all night listening to my fears.

"If you really loved me you'd know what I want without me having to tell you."

PARENT TO CHILD:
"If you're not a brilliant, perfectly obedient and organized person, I cannot love you."

"If you just try hard enough, you can achieve anything I want you to achieve. If not, you are worthless in my eyes."

"The greatest crime is to be average."

"Boys, play quietly and don't fight for the next two hours so I can sleep."

PARENT TO THREE-YEAR-OLD:
"You must never spill or make a mess."

"You must not wear out your shoes; they must last a full year."

TO LEARNING-DISABLED CHILD:
"I expect you to get 100% on every test."

"Stop fidgeting and concentrate!"

☞ **FOR PERFECTIONISTS:**
Unrealistic demands lead to a chronic sense of disappointment and bitterness. Work to accept Hashem's will, so that you will not hurt others with angry words or gestures when they fail to live up to your demands. There is only one Perfect: God. By constantly pointing out others' failings, you are displaying your own major imperfection, i.e., your failure to love.

☞ **FOR VICTIMS:**
God values effort. Do your best for your sake. Don't try to please perfectionists. This is impossible, for they are unpleasable.

14. DENYING THE WRONGDOING OR THE REALITY: Denying the truth is one of the most crazy-making behaviors of all. There is "innocent denial" based on naiveté and excessive optimism, as in those who say, "There is no physical or emotional abuse in our community." But many people deny wrongdoing as a habit, insisting, "I don't know what you're talking about." They also attack the person who dares to speak the truth. The more disturbed the abuser is, the more outrageous the denial will be.

> **HUSBAND TO WIFE:**
> "My child has no learning disabilities! I don't care if he can't read, is disturbing his teacher, provoking his peers and can't concentrate. He's just lazy and stubborn!"
>
> "I don't have a drinking problem. I just need to relax."

WIFE TO HUSBAND:
"We have no marital problems! Our marriage is fine! You're just crazy. Go into any house in the neighborhood and you'll find out that I'm the best spouse around."

"I don't overspend. I need all this jewelry to make me feel better."

ANYONE TO ANYONE:
"I don't have an anger problem. If people would stop provoking me, I'd be fine."

People with APD will lie and simply rewrite history:

"It never happened. You just have a victim mentality."

"You were the one who did it. You're hallucinating again."

☞ **FOR VICTIMS:**
There is nothing more crazy-making than making you think that what happened didn't happen. It is dangerous to be around such people. You cannot force a person to see the truth. Talking to them will only make you feel crazier.

15. DISCRIMINATING AGAINST WHOLE GROUPS: Our urge to hurt others is often justified as legitimate by adopting a negative attitude toward an entire group of people.

"We don't want you in our school/group because you're a *ba'al teshuvah*/divorced/have a handicapped child/Sephardic/Ashkenazic, Zionist/anti-Zionist, Chassidic/non-Chassidic, etc."

☞ FOR PREJUDICED PEOPLE:

Your constant judging distances you from God. Avoid condemning whole groups of people.

16. DISRESPECTING OTHERS: There are any number of ways to express disrespect for others. While such behavior may not be classified as true *ona'as devarim*, it certainly shows poor manners.

TOWARD SPOUSE:

ও Making a joke out of a mistake or failure in a scornful manner.

ও Laughing off his or her advice as stupid.

ও Correcting him or her in public.

ও Constantly belittling him for not making enough money.

TOWARD PARENTS:

ও Saying, "Get off my back" or "I'm not your slave" when they ask for something.

ও Deliberately ignoring them.

ও Not paying attention when they talk to you.

ও Having a fit when they say you cannot have what you want.

ও Mentioning their handicaps and weaknesses.

TOWARD FAMILY MEMBERS:

ও Making disparaging comments about family members in their presence, especially concerning their failures or handicaps.

- Non-verbal forms of disrespect, such as: gabbing with friends after shul while the family waits for Kiddush; ignoring the presence of others at the table by reading or talking on the phone; walking away when someone is talking.

- Implying to parents or in-laws, "We don't want a relationship; we just want your money."

Toward teachers:

- Laughing at the way the teacher dresses or talks, or laughing at a mistake s/he made.

- Talking with friends in the middle of class.

- Inciting peers by saying, "Oh good, we have a substitute! Now we can be wild!"

Toward anyone:

- Interrupting someone in the middle of a sentence.

- Rushing others unnecessarily, impatiently saying "Nu, already" or "Hurry up!" when rushing is totally unnecessary. Or saying, "Talk fast — I have more important things to do than to listen to you."

- Saying, "Forget it — you wouldn't understand anyway."

- Making a joke after someone has made a serious comment.

- Careless or irresponsible actions, such as: not returning borrowed items promptly, not bathing frequently, not brushing one's teeth, leaving dirty clothing on the floor, not cleaning up after oneself after eating or bathing, ignoring others when help is needed, singing when someone is studying, making unnecessary noise, etc. It is also disrespectful to read others' mail, listen to their phone conversations or go through their belongings without their permission.

☞ **FOR VICTIMS:**
Be firm about what you like and don't like. Say, "I will not allow you to act like this." Repeat your request in a firm, but respectful voice. Remember, good manners should be demonstrated regardless of others' bad manners.

17. DIVERTING ATTENTION: To get themselves off the hook, an offender may engage in diversionary tactics, such as:

> **DISCREDITING YOU:**
> "You're just a woman/not a rabbi/not *frum* from birth, so you don't have any right to say anything."
>
> "You went to a therapist/rabbi and spoke *lashon hara* about me and that makes you the sinner."
>
> "You are just an X type of person and that means you have nothing of value to say."
>
> **DISCREDITING THE INFORMATION:**
> "You say that hostility is harmful to the immune system? Where did you read that? You should know that you can't trust scientists."
>
> "I'll quote ten *gemaras* which disprove your *gemara*!"

Accusing you of being influenced by outsiders when you refuse to take abuse:

"You never complained before. Who turned you against me? I'll get him!" [*Note*: This often occurs when a previously passive, unconfident victim begins to gain a degree of self-respect.]

Minimizing the event:

"So I hit you. Big deal. It's over. Why do you keep bringing up the past? The whole problem is you. If you were really spiritual, you would forgive and forget."

Questioning your legitimate suspicions toward someone known to be untrustworthy:

"Why don't you trust me? Maybe you have an emotional problem!"

Counter-accusing:

"So what if I exploded? You can't even keep the house in order!"

Quibbling over some minor detail:

"You said I hit you on Monday morning when it was actually Monday afternoon. That proves that you don't know what you're talking about."

"I never called you a liar. I just said you distort the truth. There's a big difference, which you are too stupid to know."

"You say I'm very critical. What do you mean by "very"? Calling me critical is *ona'as devarim*. So you're the sinner!"

☞ **For victims:**

Say, "I was hurt. That is the only point I want to focus on.

I have the right to live in a home free of terror."

18. DOMINATING IN A DICTATORIAL MANNER: Obviously, there are times when authoritative orders must be given, especially to children and in times of stress. However, some people enjoy the role of petty tyrant, habitually barking out orders when doing so is not necessary, to deprive others of their sense of identity, individuality and freedom of thought and action. When a decision needs to be made, they do not allow for the processing stage in which ideas are floated and pros and cons considered. Rather, they quickly and impulsively decide on the basis of what is in their own best interests, ignoring the needs and feelings of everyone else concerned.

> WIFE TO HUSBAND:
> "I demand full use of the credit card with no restrictions."
>
> "I don't care if you're in debt; the house needs a full renovation."
>
> "I don't care how tired you are, do this errand."
>
> HUSBAND TO WIFE:
> "Bring me food immediately!"
>
> "I don't allow you to fix anything that breaks. You'll have to manage until I get around to fixing it, no matter how long it takes."
>
> "My mother is coming to stay with us and that's final!"
>
> "To be considered a 'kosher wife,' you must do as I say. I do not allow you to make the smallest decision without my permission, whether it

means spending a dollar, leaving the house for any reason or talking to anyone I do not approve of, and at the moment I do not approve of anyone you know."

"You can't have a checking account or a credit card. I don't care how frugal you are, it's not good enough for me." (*Note*: Of course, if the person is really not trustworthy, then this is a wise move.)

PARENT TO CHILD:
"You'll wear the clothes I choose for you, even if no one else in your class wears clothes like these.

"You'll eat what I tell you to eat, even if you hate it."

"I don't care if you're sick. You're going to school!"

CHILD TO CHILD:
"I'm older, so you have to do whatever I say."

19. EMBARRASSING OTHERS: All *ona'as devarim* involves shaming others. This is especially damaging when a person is shamed for acts which are not under his conscious control, such as gender, personality, intelligence, handicaps, racial origin, etc.

CHILD TO CHILD:
"You only got 60% on the test?"

"Does it bother you to have so many freckles?"

"You're adopted!"

"We have a nickname for you!"

PARENT TO CHILD:
"I'm telling all the guests that you still wet your bed."

"Such a dummy God gave me for a child!"

"Keep eating and you won't fit through the door."

"Stop being so emotional/shy/hyper/immature."
[*Note*: These traits are not under our conscious control.]

TEACHER TO CHILD:
"Is this how your mother sends you to school?"

"Anyone who didn't finish copying from the board/didn't do the homework must stand in the corner."

"You need to go to the bathroom now? What a baby! You can't even wait! Bring a diaper to school tomorrow."

"That was such a stupid answer!"

TO A PERSON WITH A HANDICAP:
"I wonder why Hashem is punishing you."

"I have a friend with exactly the same condition you have and you'd never guess there's anything wrong with her."

ANYONE TO ANYONE:
"I've heard that you're having problems." (Said in a superior, unsympathetic tone of voice.)

When a person uses words to embarrass by association (indirect mud-slinging), you may not realize that it's still offensive:

"At least you're not as crazy as your mother."

"Thank God your nutty divorced sister isn't coming to visit."

A mother with APD might say to her child,

"You inherited stupid genes from your father's side of the family. You're such a disappointment to me. I'm ashamed that you're my child."

20. IGNORING OR EXCLUDING OTHERS: Technically, ignoring others or giving them the silent treatment is not *ona'as devarim*, since nothing has been said. However, not showing any interest in others, not asking about their health and welfare, gives the message that they are insignificant. Treating someone as if he is insignificant or invisible is one of the most painful things that can be done to a person. (This does not apply in the case of a victim who must ignore an abusive person to protect his/her sanity.) Also, excluding a person intentionally, with him knowing you are doing it, hurts.

      ᗛ A spouse uses the silent treatment as a punishment to get his/her way.

      ᗛ A child is ignored because he does not live up to the parents' expectations.

      ᗛ The teacher only calls on the bright children and ignores those who are slower.

      ᗛ At a social event, you are deliberately snubbed

because you belong to the "wrong" side of the family or don't follow their lifestyle.

ଔ In the middle of dinner, the wife answers the phone and chats away, ignoring her husband and children.

ଔ The patient asks his hospital roommate to lower the volume on the radio and is ignored.

ଔ An in-law telephones and asks for the person from his or her side of the family while ignoring your existence.

Another form of ignoring is to exclude others solely for the reason that they lack status.

ଔ Inviting all the well-to-do family members for an occasion and not the poor ones.

Children, in particular, can be very cruel when they exclude others. They may invite all the children to a party except one or two, or say, "We don't want you in our group. You're fat and you stink and you're cross-eyed. Besides, your parents aren't frum enough/are immigrants/etc."

☞ **FOR VICTIMS OF SNUB:**
Parents can help their children make new friends. You can create a new "family" of friends who love and value you as you are, especially people who have also suffered from abuse and are looking for nurturing relationships. Imagine! You can pick your own compatible parents, siblings and children.

EXPLOITING: This is when you ask another person to do something that you really don't even need, just to make him or her serve you.

HUSBAND TO WIFE (who just sat down after being on her feet all day):
"Bring me a cup of coffee."

WIFE TO HUSBAND (who just came home):
"Run to the store; I have a sudden craving for X." [*Note*: Even reasonable requests can become *ona'as devarim* when used to control another person.]

MOTHER TO FRIEND (shmoozing over coffee):
"I'm sure my neighbor won't mind if I don't pick up my kids on time. She loves children."

BABYSITTER TO FRIEND:
"I'm sure the people I'm babysitting for won't mind if I talk on their phone for hours and eat whatever's in the fridge."

☞ **FOR VICTIMS:**
Do not help others if doing so hurts you.

22. EXCUSING HARMFUL BEHAVIOR BY BLAMING OTHERS (SCAPEGOATING): Ask any young child why he hit his friend, and he is likely to say, "'Cause he hit me." Immature people will use this same "excuse mentality" to blame others for their irresponsibility, outbursts and bad manners, thus promoting the following lies:

"I can't help it if I neglect my children. I wasn't cut out to be a parent. Anyway, I don't like their personality."

"When I'm tired, nervous, or hungry, I don't have to control myself! In fact, if anyone bothers me at these times, it's their own fault if they get blasted!"

"You hurt me, so that means I can hurt you back."

"I have to yell/hit because: it's the only way to get my kids up in the morning/get them dressed/get them to eat/get them to learn/get them to cooperate/get them to clean up/get them to bed. They're wild animals."

"I can't control myself. I'm a hot-tempered person by nature."

"I'm mean and irresponsible because I had a bad childhood."

"I wasn't loved as a child, so I can't be a loving person now."

CX *"My son accidentally spilled his juice while eating. He then yelled at his sister, 'Stupid! It's all your fault. You made me nervous.' I immediately explained that he spilled it by mistake and there was no need to blame anyone."*

☞ **FOR EXCUSERS:**
The basis for addictive behavior is self-justification. Drinkers, smokers and overeaters as well as "rage-aholics" (those with explosive tempers) all excuse their destructive behavior as unavoidable. Maturity means taking responsibility for your behavior and facing disappointments with faith and positive action. Are you ready?

Learn the difference between an excuse and a reason:

CX A reason for not cleaning up your home might be a 104°-fever. An excuse is, "I wasn't in the mood."

ଓ A reason for depression might be a tragic loss, God forbid. An excuse is, "I didn't get anything new for the holidays."

ଓ A reason for not getting to work on time might be a massive traffic jam. An excuse is, "I just couldn't get out of bed."

ଓ A reason for not looking for a job might be a broken leg. An excuse is, "Schedules make me feel stifled."

ଓ A reason for screaming is an immediate danger to one's life. An excuse is, "I don't have the will power to control myself."

Bad moods are no excuse for bad manners! Don't look for excuses to lose control or be irresponsible. Be extra cautious about what you say to others when you are fatigued, hungry or irritable. Don't be lazy; take responsibility for your manners and *middos*.

ଓ Read my book, *Raising Children to Care*,[*] to learn non-hostile methods of getting children to cooperate and develop good *middos*.

☞ **FOR VICTIMS:**
Don't take responsibility for other people's moods or *middos*! If you do, they won't.

23. EXPLODING ANGRILY: In *Sefer Yere'im* 170, we are told not to frighten people with an angry face. An angry explosion is like being under Katyusha rocket attack. Living with someone who tends to explode is like living in a war zone. Even if the bombs fall only occasionally, you can

_____

* Feldheim Publishers.

never relax, since you never know when the next one will hit. A person who explodes angrily at frequent intervals teaches family members to lie, since they will do so in the hope of avoiding another explosion. Then the exploder gets angrier when he discovers the deception, leading to more dishonesty.

One is not allowed to speak in a way which alarms or distresses others. With children, a parent may wear a "mask" of anger, only if he does not truly feel angry! (Rambam, *Hilchos De'os* 7:5, 2:3).

☞ **FOR EXPLODERS:**
The following will help — if you want help:

> ☙ If you feel bad about your bad temper, that is a positive sign! Look into the different options available for helping you to control your temper. Consider this to be your first step.

> ☙ No doubt, you have an "excuse mentality," which means you believe you have the right to explode whenever a family member displeases you. This is a dangerous, abusive mind-set which must be changed. No doubt, you learned in childhood that raging at others is normal, acceptable and inevitable. It isn't! Get help to change your thinking.

> ☙ Join a support group. You must discover how to reconnect with your lost ability to love others, to forgive and express compassion on a consistent basis. You are locked into negative habits just like an alcoholic. Effective rehabilitation programs exist. EMETT tools are excellent for defusing anger.

ରେ Strengthen your faith in God. If someone hurts you, remember: "One does not hurt his finger in this world unless it has been decreed from Above" (*Chullin* 7b). Tell yourself over and over, "There is a reason for this hurt. God is giving me a chance to improve my *middos* — forgiveness, respect compassion, patience, etc. My behavior must be independent of theirs. I can be a *mentsch* even if others disappoint me or misbehave." Keep saying these words over and over until they become an *automatic* response.

ରେ Consider taking medication to control your outbursts.

ରେ Realize that anger may stop certain behavior temporarily but doesn't change people on any deep level. In fact, anger strengthens the very behavior you dislike since people become defiant to protect their independence, integrity and identity.

ରେ If you feel you must scream, scream something positive, such as, "Thank you for giving me the opportunity to work on my *middos*." Or, "God! Give me strength to stay civilized!"

☞ **FOR VICTIMS:**
Do not blame yourself, unless you have been deliberately obnoxious. Insist that the person get professional help. Sadly, abusers do not seek help since they think nothing is wrong with them. You will need a lot of support to stay sane.

24. FANTASIZING VERBALLY IN A WAY WHICH MAKES OTHERS ANXIOUS OR RAISES THEIR HOPES IN VAIN:

To Spouse:
"What would life have been like if I'd married someone else?"

"How would you feel if I decided I didn't want to be frum?"

Husband who lacks business acumen to wife:
"I'm thinking of borrowing half a million dollars and starting my own business."

Wife to financially strained husband:
"We simply must rip out this old kitchen and get a new one just like our neighbors."

To storeowner:
"How much is that item?" (If the person has no intention of buying it.)

Anyone to anyone:
"I'll kill myself if the project doesn't work out."

☞ For fantasizers:
Warn the other person first that what you are about to discuss is only a fantasy. Or, keep it to yourself.

25. Forcing others to beg by withholding what they need: Children who crave a sense of power and control will sometimes refuse to cooperate in order to force parents into the humiliating position of having to beg them to eat, get dressed, go to school or clean up their messes. Some never outgrow this habit. They become difficult adults who get perverse pleasure out of withholding whatever others want, whether it is affection, time, money, food or assistance. A nurse may ignore a patient's urgent calls for help, an employer may withhold his workers' wages, a wife may

never find time to listen to her husband's feelings, a husband may say he will pay a doctor's bill, but never gets around to it, thus forcing both the doctor's secretary and the wife to beg.

The "Let them beg" attitude is a form of emotional cruelty. However, since no active aggression is involved, the withholder can claim to be innocent of all wrongdoing. Those who are dependent on withholders for physical, emotional or financial needs find that their pent-up frustration can turn into explosive rage. This makes the withholder even more obstinate about not "giving in." It is no wonder that a sane person can feel so "crazy" around a chronic withholder, since there is no way to reach such a person. It is even more frustrating if the person who is so withholding at home displays generosity to outsiders. This intensifies the suffering of those who are chronically deprived of their needs.

BARGAINING: Children often do this with parents, as in:

"I'll go to school only if you get me my own telephone line."

"I'll take out the garbage if you pay me."

"I'll do the dishes if you let me have the car tonight."

WHINING:
"But I hate taking baths/cleaning my room/eating with a fork/going to school/going to work every day."

EXCUSING:
"I just didn't have the energy to do chores."

POSTPONING:
"I'll do it later."

PROCRASTINATING:
"I told you weeks ago that I'd spend time with you when I get a break from work. Now leave me alone!"

"I told you a year ago that I'd fix it when I get time. I haven't had the time. Stop nagging."

"I told you a month ago that I'd mail the mortgage along with the insurance payment. Get off my back."

"I'll get a job if something good falls in my lap."

☞ **FOR THOSE WHO CAN'T GET OTHERS TO COOPERATE WITHOUT BEGGING:**
Be firm with children. Train them to do chores from an early age. If you are too soft-hearted, others will take advantage of you and become selfish and lazy. Use charts and prizes if necessary and follow through on your demands. You are doing them a big favor by training them to be considerate of others and to function with discomfort.

Some people enjoy making others beg, sometimes for the basic necessities of life, such as food, money, clothing or affection. They may provoke their victim to explode or be in total despair, and only then put up the shelf or provide a bit of affection and even then do it reluctantly. Irresponsible adults almost invite nagging by their refusal to bathe, clean up after themselves, keep a job or keep their promises. This is a severe emotional disturbance which requires professional help.

26. FAVORITISM: Since the time of our Patriarch Yaakov,

parents have been warned by our Sages not to single out one child for preferential treatment because of the pain this causes others. This is true also of teachers and their "pets."

27. GESTURING WITH CONTEMPT: This is a deliberate act which humiliates or shames others. It radiates contempt and disgust. A Torah-true Jew should work to control his urge to hurt others. These gestures include:

> ❧ Rolling your eyes when someone states an opinion.

> ❧ Turning your back on someone.

> ❧ Sighing with exasperation, looking frequently at your watch or at the clock, or looking bored when the person talks.

> ❧ Putting your hands over your ears when a parent talks.

> ❧ Dismissing a person with a contemptuous wave of the hand.

> ❧ Motioning in a circle with your pointer finger at the side of your head to indicate that the other person is crazy.

If you tell someone with APD what bothers you, they will do it even more often.

☞ **FOR VICTIMS:**
Stop communicating with such a person, the sooner, the better. Trying to "win them over" will usually only subject you to more abuse. Feel good about not responding. This will leave you feeling empowered. Learn to quickly and

forcefully divert your attention to other matters. Find ful-filling outside activities and friends to help you stay sane.

28. GIVING UNSOLICITED ADVICE in a way which insults the person's intelligence or makes light of the problem:

> TO THE PARENT OF A LEARNING-DISABLED CHILD:
> "There's nothing wrong with that kid that a few good whacks won't solve."

> TO A PERSON WITH AN ABUSIVE FAMILY MEMBER:
> "Just do his will, no matter how crazy it seems."

> "Just don't take it to heart."

> "You can choose not to feel hurt."

> "Just don't take this craziness. Stand up for your-self."

> "You just need to find the right words and s/he will stop." [*Note*: Outsiders assume that victims have more power than they really have and that abusers are far more reasonable and pleasable than they are.]

> TO A PERSON WITH A SERIOUS ILLNESS:
> "Just go on a macrobiotic diet/to my homeo-path/doctor/chiropractor/reflexologist, etc. and you'll be fine."

> "You mustn't go to doctors. Just have faith."

> TO AN OVERWEIGHT PERSON:
> "I'm going to grab the food out of your hands whenever I see you eating anything fattening."

TO A PERSON WITH EMOTIONAL PROBLEMS:
"Just stop feeling sorry for yourself."

"Just think positively."

TO A NEW MOTHER:
"Don't give a pacifier."

"Don't feed so often. She'll get fat."

"Don't hold her so much. She'll get spoiled."

"Just let him cry."

TO A SMALL CHILD WHO IS BEING PICKED ON BY A BULLY:
"Go over and punch him in the nose." [Note: Asking a sensitive child to fight a bully without giving your child lessons in self-defense is putting him in a suicidal position. The police or other authorities should be called in immediately.]

TO AN UNMARRIED PERSON:
"You're too picky. Time is racing by and you're not getting any younger, so you'd better compromise."

"Don't let your date know what you're really like."

"If you really wanted to get married, you would."

"Your time will come. Don't you worry."

TO A PERSON WITH PROBLEMATIC TEENAGERS:
"Just throw them out of the house. That'll teach them."

Back-Seat Driving is another annoying type of advice-giving. This can take place in the kitchen, car or any other place and involves a more-or-less continuous stream of confidence-wrecking comments: Don't go into that lane/don't pass that car/don't put the blinker on yet/you can get a better parking space/the baby needs socks/now she's too warm/take the socks off/she's hungry/you're feeding her too much/you're holding her too tight/you're pampering her/she'll be spoiled/pick her up, she's feeling neglected.

☞ **FOR ADVICE GIVERS:**
Before you offer advice, ask the person, "Would you like my advice about that?" Be aware that your advice may convey the hidden message: "You're too inept to find your own solutions."

☞ **FOR VICTIMS:**
Say, "Thank you for the suggestion." "It's being taken care of." "Trust me to make good decisions."

29. GUILT-TRIPPING: This happens when a person unreasonably blames others for his lack of health and happiness.

> **PARENT TO CHILD:**
> "It's all your fault that I: Had a nervous breakdown/Lost my job/Am totally unhappy/Am always sick."
>
> "If you don't do as I want, I'll have a heart attack and die."
>
> "I could have had a much happier life if you hadn't been born. I could be rich by now."
>
> "I don't care how abused you are. If you go

ahead and get divorced, I'll die."

BUSINESSMAN OR PROFESSIONAL TO RELATIVE:
"I'm terribly offended that you used someone else's services. You should have given your business to a family member."

When one person threatens to stop loving another over his lack of compliance, this is emotional blackmail!

PARENT TO GROWN-UP CHILD:
"If you don't give the baby the name I want, I won't come to the *bris*."

CHILD TO PARENT:
"But all the other kids have it/do it."

"If I can't have a $50,000 wedding, I won't get married!"

TO A FAMILY MEMBER:
"If you don't get me what I want, I'll get depressed/get sick/die."

☞ **FOR GUILT-TRIPPERS:**
Take responsibility for your own happiness and *middos*.

☞ **FOR VICTIMS:**
Don't take responsibility for other people's unhappiness unless you have been purposely hurtful toward them.

30. INVALIDATING/TRIVIALIZING EMOTIONS: Telling people that it is wrong to feel what they feel makes their pain more intense.

PARENT TO CHILD (who is afraid or in pain):
"There's nothing to be scared of. Don't you

know that big boys don't cry."

"It's nothing. Stop being such a baby."

"It doesn't hurt."

PRINCIPAL TO PARENT (who complains of an abusive teacher):
"You're exaggerating. No one else has complained."

HUSBAND TO CRITICIZED WIFE (who says she feels unloved):
"I do love you. I only criticize you to show how much I care."

"I didn't hurt you. I can't talk to you any more, you're so touchy. You can't take criticism! You're crazy!"

DOCTOR OR NURSE TO PATIENT:
"Stop screaming. You know it doesn't really hurt. No one else ever had such a response. Everyone's looking at you."

TO SOMEONE WHO IS CRYING OVER A LOST LOVED ONE:
"Stop that right now! He wouldn't have wanted to see you crying."

"Don't cry — it will make his spirit sad. Be happy that he is at peace and together with Hashem now."

"Stop feeling sorry for yourself."

"If you cry, it means you have no faith."

TO SOMEONE WHO ISN'T CRYING OVER A LOST LOVED ONE:
"Why aren't you crying? Don't you care?"

TO SOMEONE YOU HAVE HURT:
"Calm down! You make a big deal about everything."

"There are institutions for people like you."

TO A PERSON IN PAIN:
"You'll get over it. It's not the end of the world."

TO SOMEONE WHO HAS UNDERGONE A TRAUMA:
"Just forget the past."

TO A CHILD WHO HAS BEEN REJECTED:
"Big deal! You'll make new friends. There are a lot worse problems."

TO A PERSON WHO HAS LOST A JOB:
"It's not the end of the world. At least you can sleep late in the morning."

TO A PARENT WHO LOST A HANDICAPPED CHILD:
"It must be a relief."

TO A CHILDLESS COUPLE:
"Just relax and everything will be fine."

"You are so lucky not to have a bunch of screaming brats yet. Enjoy your freedom."

TO A CHILD WHO WAS REJECTED BY THE SCHOOL HE APPLIED TO:
"Don't take it so hard. There are a lot of other schools around."

☞ **FOR SUPPRESSORS:**
Everyone has his own emotional truth. Trying to argue with that truth only hurts people's feelings and increases the intensity of the suppressed feelings.

Practice becoming a *nosei b'ol* — a person who can empathize with those in pain. Say, "It's tough. I'm sorry you're in pain. Tell me more about it. What does this loss mean to you?" LISTEN. LISTENING IS LOVE.

Also, remember the advice of our Sages not to comfort a person at the height of his pain (*Avos* 4:18).

☞ **FOR VICTIMS:**
Remember that it is difficult for people to understand and empathize unless they've been through the same experience. You can sometimes teach others how to empathize. Otherwise, confide only in those who have had similar experiences.

31. ISOLATING: Overly possessive types will often try to isolate family members by forbidding outside activities and friendships even with family members, in the vain hope that this will make them feel more secure. Bullies do this to gain more control.

> TO SPOUSE:
> "Your relatives/friends are crazy/not frum enough/too frum. I don't want them around. You're not allowed to have anything to do with them."
>
> "You can't leave the house without my permission."
>
> "I don't want you going to classes. I'm lonely without you here."

"What do you need friends for? You have me!"

PARENT TO CHILD:
"You don't need to play with friends in the afternoon. You can see them in school."

32. JOKING/TEASING/RIDICULING/BEING SARCASTIC:

JOKING AT OTHER PEOPLE'S EXPENSE:
"We call her Bernie 'cause she's always burning the food."

"Nice outfit you're wearing, ha-ha." (To someone who is wearing an old shabby outfit.)

"You open your mouth to switch feet, ha-ha!"

"Here's the health-food nut with his health foods."

"Oh, you finally decided to lift a finger? Hope you don't get cramps from working so hard."

"Not again! You had the same problem last month!"

TEASING PEOPLE ABOUT THEIR WEAKNESSES:
"Fatso is chomping away again."

"The genius has made a really profound comment."

MIMICKING PEOPLE'S HANDICAPS, SUCH AS A LIMP OR STUTTER.

MAKING PRACTICAL JOKES AT THE EXPENSE OF OTHERS, SUCH AS CALLING SOMEONE'S HOME

AND ASKING FOR A PIZZA DELIVERY.

33. KICKING PEOPLE WHEN THEY'RE ALREADY DOWN: When some people see that another person is down, they cannot control the urge to make the person feel even worse. This urge to gloat over another's failure is a sign of spiritual failure.

> **ADULT TO CHILD** (who has just fallen):
> "I told you not to run! Stop crying or I'll give you something to really cry about."

> **TO A PERSON WHO HAS LOST SOMETHING:**
> "If you weren't such a scatter-brain, you wouldn't have lost it."

> **TO A PERSON YOU HAVE JUST INSULTED:**
> "I didn't hurt you. You just can't take criticism. You're too sensitive."

> **TO A PERSON WHO HAS JUST LOST MONEY:**
> "I told you not to invest in that company! Why didn't you listen to me?"

> **TO A PERSON WHO FAILED:**
> "Stupid! I told you so. It's your own fault."

> **TO ANYONE:**
> "Why didn't you think about it beforehand?"

> "If I were you, I would have..."

34. LYING: Although they may try not to, most people will, at times, say something that is not true, even if the lie is merely exaggerating the number of people who attended a simchah or giving a false excuse about missing an appointment or a day of work. Lying is especially dam-

aging when it involves:

> ೞ Lying about people's character, as in *shidduchim*, where negative information may be withheld in the mistaken notion that "everything will turn out just fine once they're married."

> ೞ Lying in order to get people to invest money in shady business deals.

> ೞ Lying about one's true feelings and needs in order to deceive others.

> ೞ Lying about having done something one didn't do.

"The check is in the mail."

"I paid the bill."

"I'll improve after we are married."

Giving Mixed Messages is a form of lying where a person says one thing while his body language conveys the opposite message. For example:

FUMING ADULT:
"I am not angry!"

CRYING PARENT:
"Everything's fine. Nothing's wrong. I'm not upset. You're imagining things."

ABUSIVE PARENT:
"I hit you so often because I love you."

☞ **FOR LIARS:**

Lying corrupts you and destroys relationships. If you are hot-tempered, you force your family members to lie to avoid getting you angry. They will lie about where they've been and what they've bought. Children will lie about their marks to avoid your anger or name-calling. They will lie about where they got candy and other possessions. They may steal because stealing is a symbolic way of getting the love they are missing.

☞ **FOR VICTIMS:**

Relationships are based on trust and honest communication. Do not expect to have a relationship with a liar.

35. MAKING PROMISES one has no intention of fulfilling or breaking promises once they have been made:

> **TO SPOUSE:**
> "You can unpack your suitcase. I've changed my mind about going on the vacation we talked about."
>
> **CHILD TO PARENT:**
> "I'll do that chore in a minute."
>
> **FRIEND TO FRIEND:**
> "I'll return the money I borrowed right away."
>
> **CONTRACTOR TO HOUSEWIFE:**
> "I'll have your new kitchen finished in a week. It'll be just what you wanted."
>
> **REPAIRMAN TO CLIENT:**
> "I'll be there first thing in the morning."
>
> **DOCTOR TO PATIENT:**
> "This operation will solve all your problems."

LAWYER TO CLIENT:
"I'll take only a small percentage."

ADVERTISER TO READER:
"Just use this product and in no time, you'll have a whole new face/personality/life."

☞ **FOR PROMISE-BREAKERS:**
Don't make promises you can't keep.

36. MONITORING/STARING/LEERING: While not technically verbal abuse, penetrating a person's personal space with one's eyes can be very distressing to them.

> ∞ Monitoring someone's actions as if s/he is under a high-powered microscope and then insulting the person. For example, inspecting the food and saying in a loud accusatory tone, "Who taught you how to cook?"

> ∞ Staring at another person's clothing or body in a way which makes him feel self-conscious or ashamed (*Orach Chayim* 170:4) and then making a comment which confirms that feeling. For example, after looking the person up and down, saying, "You'd better go on a diet."

> ∞ Leering at someone in a way that shows contempt or as a way of frightening him/her (*Choshen Mishpat* 420:32) is forbidden. Even without the addition of words, just misusing the eyes can cause emotional pain.

37. NAGGING/LECTURING: It is expected that children will nag for what they want, especially those with aggressive personalities. If parents fail to respond with firm limits, children may grow up to be tyrannical adults who control

others through force.

Of course, it is the responsibility of parents and teachers to persist in helping children overcome negative habits. This duty goes beyond normal bounds when force is used to fulfill the needs of the parent while the rights and needs of the child are ignored.

The urge to fix, mold and change others is a sign of deep-seated anxiety and dependency. The more a nagger nags or a lecturer lectures, the more resistant others become, which makes naggers and lecturers even more determined to get their way.

> TO SPOUSE:
> "I've told you a million times to lose weight/keep the towels straight/never waste a penny."

> CHILD TO PARENT:
> "I'm going to keep asking until you let me have what I want!"

> PARENT TO CHILD:
> "I've told you a million times to take your thumb out of your mouth/clean your room/stand up straight/keep your elbows off the table/chew your food slowly."

> TO LEARNING-DISABLED CHILD:
> "I've told you a million times to concentrate/ stop fidgeting/get organized!"

☞ FOR NAGGERS:
If you are turning into a nag, something is wrong. Learn positive communication tactics. For example:

> ❧ Make sure the person is capable of making

the change you want, in terms of his level of intelligence and God-given nature.

ଔ Look at the person to whom you are talking. If you see the fog roll into his eyes when you open your mouth, talking will be counter-productive. The major difference between a reminder and harassment is the number of times you repeat the request and the tone of your voice. A reminder is said in a friendly voice, without judgment or impatience.

ଔ Don't fall for excuses. If the person says, "when I get around to it," pin him down to a specific time and date and state a consequence if it doesn't get done. Mark it on your calendar. Say, "Tell me what words I can use that will get you to pay the bill/get a job/not leave your dirty laundry on the floor, etc."

ଔ If you know that a child's "later" really means "never," state rules firmly but calmly. "You can play after you do your homework/clean up your room." There is a saying that "A lazy mother picks up after her children." Don't do it!

ଔ Be aware that excessive nagging undermines a child's self-worth. He'll defy you just not to give you the satisfaction of getting your way.

ଔ Over the next few months build up your relationship by keeping the praise-to-criticism ratio around twenty-to-one. Then the person may be receptive to occasional rebuke.

ଔ If an adult is so indifferent or irresponsible that s/he will not bathe, work or assume minimal obligations, nagging will not help. Instead of being chronically resentful, find fulfilling activities which nourish your soul in a way which the people around you may not be able to do. Your broken dreams are no excuse to stay miserable.

38. NAME-CALLING: A spiritually elevated person loves God and loves His creations (*Pirkei Avos* 6:1); he finds name-calling repulsive. Name-calling or giving people nicknames to tease them is *ona'as devarim*.

HUSBAND TO WIFE:
"Crazy! You're just hysterical over nothing!"

PARENT TO CHILD:
"Fatso! Stop eating so much."

"Stupid. Retarded idiot! Look at these marks!"

"Lazy bums! Look at this mess!"

"I could kill you, you no-good brats."

"You whiney pest! Get away from me!"

"Idiot! How could you lose your keys!"

☞ **FOR NAME-CALLERS:**
Don't do it! Ever. It's always counter-productive and encourages the very behavior you want to stop! A label reinforces the other person's feeling, "I really am awful, so why even try to be good?" It's low-level to focus on people's weaknesses and even more low-level to constantly point them out.

39. NEGLECTING: Neglecting the physical or emotional

needs of family members is one of the most devastating forms of abuse. Nothing hurts more than to feel "No one cares about me." Children and spouses may be driven to suicidal despair.

TO SPOUSE:
"Leave me alone! I don't have time for you!"

PARENT TO CHILD:
"Shut up. Get away. You're nothing but a pest."

"I don't care if you are failing in school. It's not my problem."

"I'm not interfering in your fights. You can kill each other. I don't care."

TEACHER TO PARENT OF A LEARNING-DISABLED CHILD:
"I don't have time to pay attention to the slow ones. They're not worth it anyway."

☞ FOR VICTIMS:
Trying to get a neglectful person to pay attention to you is like sucking on an empty bottle. You'll end up frustrated and furious. Seek out people who appreciate you.

40. PATRONIZING is speaking to another person as if he is unintelligent:

HUSBAND TO WIFE:
"This is something a woman wouldn't understand."

PARENT TO CHILD:
"You're just a child, so don't ask questions."

DOCTOR OR NURSE TO PATIENT:
"Don't worry. These anti-depressants have no side-effects." [*Note*: All anti-depressants have side effects.]

41. POISONING ONE PERSON AGAINST ANOTHER: It is common for people to want others to dislike those people whom *they* dislike, as a way of justifying their resentments:

PARENT TO CHILD:
"Don't listen to your mother/father. S/he doesn't know what s/he's talking about. S/he is crazy."

CLASSMATE TO CLASSMATE:
"Don't consider her for a *shidduch*. Her parents are divorced."

"She has a retarded brother."

ABOUT A STUDENT:
"Don't bother investing time in him. He'll never amount to anything."

ABOUT A NEIGHBOR:
"I'd look elsewhere for friendship if I were you." (Unless, of course, the warning is necessary.)

42. PUNISHING UNFAIRLY: Few realize that in "spare the rod, spoil the child" (*Mishlei* 13:24), "rod" means a staff such as shepherds use to protect and herd sheep gently, but firmly, in the right direction. Cruelty does not educate. Cruelty teaches children to be cruel.

PARENT TO CHILD:
"You won't move from the table until you finish your meal. I don't care if you have to sit there all day."

"I'll take away your favorite toy for a month.
Each time you disobey, I'll add another month."

"No desserts for the next three months."

A parent with APD might tell a child, "I'll beat you until you learn to obey." A husband might tell his wife, "Because you disobeyed, you won't get any grocery money." A wife might tell her husband, "I'm not talking to you for the next month."

TO SPOUSE:
"Since you hurt my feelings, you will pay for it for the rest of your life."

☞ **FOR PUNISHERS:**
Overly harsh punishments invariably cause others to hate you and seek revenge, often by repeating the same behavior you punished. Thus, excessive punishment can be considered a violation of the prohibition, "Do not put a stumbling block before the blind" (*Vayikra* 19:14). Join a group, attend parenting classes or seek professional advice to learn to overcome this destructive habit.

43. QUESTIONING/INTERROGATING TO ANNOY OR HUMILIATE:

ASKING NOSY QUESTIONS:
"How did you buy an apartment on a *kollel* salary?"

"Why did you get divorced?"

"How come you're still single?"

"Why isn't your daughter married yet?"

☞ **FOR VICTIMS:**

Say, "Thank you for your interest, but this is my own personal business." Or, reply with the question, "Why do you ask?" Or, "I can forgive you for asking if you can forgive me for not answering."

> **ASKING QUESTIONS YOU KNOW THE PERSON CAN-NOT ANSWER:**
> A teacher might embarrass a child by doing this in class.

An over-controlling husband might interrogate his wife in a manner which implies that she is totally untrustworthy, such as by going through the supermarket purchases, commenting scornfully on each one — "We don't need this! You spent so much on that?" Or, going through a list of phone calls or checks and demanding an explanation for each one, while she is required to sit before him, terrified.

44. SPYING IN ORDER TO ACCUSE OTHERS: Going through people's drawers and pockets, listening in on conversations, reading letters, and then accusing others of being untrustworthy.

☞ **FOR SPIES:**

When you keep implying that another person cannot be trusted, that person is bound to feel discouraged and will probably do something eventually to justify your suspicions. To build trust, comment positively when others are on time, when they do fulfill their promises to you and do act in a trustworthy manner. This will build a more positive atmosphere.

Paranoia stems from the inability to trust your parents during your first years of life. It is a serious problem. Get professional help.

☞ **FOR VICTIMS:**

Let others know — very firmly — what your boundaries are. However, an abusive type will not care about your feelings.

45. STINGINESS: While frugality is a good trait, stinginess implies contempt, telling others, "You're too insignificant to receive more than crumbs (if that)," or "You're bad for not being able to get by with less." Stingy people criticize others for their wastefulness:

> **TO SPOUSE:**
> "I don't care if you're freezing — we don't need the heat on!" (In the summer: "You can't put the air conditioner on.")
>
> "Why are these leftovers in the garbage? You could have used them for something!"
>
> "You could have worn that shirt another day instead of wasting water and detergent to clean it!"
>
> "Don't invite guests — they waste our money."
>
> "Don't use the phone. Keeping in touch with people isn't important. Anyway, you'll see them next year."

Stingy people also withhold their affection, time and energy, refusing to share information, ideas and feelings. Every request is met with a grouchy refusal.

46. THREATENING: This is used by people who don't have enough influence over others to suit them. They stoop to making threats in order to frighten others and gain an illusion of having power.

TO SPOUSE:
"I'll kidnap the children. You'll never see them again."

"I'll ruin you financially."

"I'll never give you a divorce. You'll be an *agunah* forever."

CHILD TO PARENT:
"If you don't give me my own phone/send me to camp/let me do what I want, I'll run away."

PARENT TO CHILD:
"I'll leave you brats and never come back!"

"I'll lock you in your room and throw away the key."

"I'll send you to an orphanage."

TO A FAMILY MEMBER:
"Get off the phone or I'll rip it out of the wall."

47. UNDERMINING THE CONFIDENCE OF OTHERS: It is very easy to undermine a person's confidence in himself.

WIFE TO HUSBAND:
"I don't expect you to amount to anything."

HUSBAND TO WIFE:
"Anything wrong with the kids is all your fault."

PARENT TO CHILD:
"Never mind. I knew I couldn't count on you."

"It's not worth helping you with your homework.

I've given up on you."

TEACHER TO CHILD:
"You'll end up sweeping the streets. You don't have the brains for anything better."

TO AN EMOTIONAL PERSON:
"Crying again? I should hospitalize you in the psychiatric ward!"

TO A PERSON WHO FORGOT:
"You forgot again? You must be losing your mind. You need to see a psychiatrist."

TO A PERSON TRYING TO LOSE WEIGHT:
"Don't even try going on a diet. You never stick to anything. You're hopeless."

TO A PERSON SEEKING A JOB:
"Don't bother looking — no one would ever hire you. You can't even keep your room in order."

TO A NEW MOTHER:
"You're feeding him too often."

"You're not feeding him often enough."

"You're spoiling the baby."

☞ **FOR VICTIMS:**
If the abuser is emotionally healthy, say, "Your words are undermining my self-confidence." If the person is emotionally disturbed, anything you say will be used to attack you once again, as such people enjoy conflict, scorning, and cruelty.

Rabbi Elazar ben Shimon said, "Just as it is a mitzvah to

say that which will be accepted, so is it a mitzvah to refrain from saying that which will not be accepted" (*Yevamos* 65b). People who lack spiritual refinement give us the opportunity to perform this mitzvah, since talking to them usually elicits more hostility. The inability to communicate with a disturbed person often makes sane people feel crazy. This is why silence and distance are often recommended.

48. USING RELIGION TO ABUSE: Spiritual health is based on feeling that God loves us and that we have a Godly essence. This bond is destroyed if God is portrayed as a kind of "monster" who is constantly enraged and who hurts people for trivial offenses, as in the words:

> "God will punish you for not eating your meal."

> "If you don't come when I call, God will cripple you."

> "God will make you go blind for looking at that."

> "If you say that, God will strike you dead."

> "God wants you to be serious. He does not want you to play."

People also inflict pain when they say to someone:

> "God hates you and that's why you got that handicap/tragedy."

Another way of using religion to abuse is giving subtle (and not so subtle) "holier than thou" messages. Some people feel that the stricter they are, the more beloved they will be by God. During any conversation, they will make a point of putting you down, by saying things like:

"We don't buy food that has the *hechsher* you use."

"I would never let my children go there."

"I would never let my children waste time with games."

A husband with APD might tell his wife, "I will adopt every religious stringency possible even if this causes you pain." Or, "If you don't meet my demands for affection, I will be forced to sin and it will be all your fault." When a woman is continually subjected to this type of coercion, the inevitable result is revulsion toward her husband.

☞ **FOR RELIGIOUS ABUSERS:**
When people feel a strong bond with a loving God, they are less likely to sin. Without love, religion becomes abusive.

49. WITHHOLDING INFORMATION THAT THE OTHER PERSON SHOULD KNOW: Silence can be a message of hostility or contempt:

> ❧ A doctor does not tell the patient about the side-effects of the medication he has prescribed or the possible after-effects of an operation he is going to perform.

> ❧ A husband does not tell his wife where he is going, when he will be home or where he gets his money from.

> ❧ A wife does not tell her husband where she has been.

> ❧ A child is not told anything about an upcoming

hospitalization, the move to a new home or other major changes, such as a family member's serious illness or death.

ᑙ A wife gets angry at her husband, but doesn't let him know why, or says, "I'm not angry. You're hallucinating." [*Note*: Double messages make people crazy!]

50. WORRYING EXCESSIVELY: Being concerned about others' welfare is a sign of love. But excessive worry conveys the message that the worrier believes the other person is inadequate and inferior, as in:

PARENT TO GROWN CHILD:
"I am so worried that you may never get married."

"I am too worried to let you handle that job on your own, even if many others your age are doing it."

"You probably won't find a job even if you take that training course! There are very few jobs around today."

"You won't know what to do when you become a parent."

"I am afraid to let you out of the house. You might see all kinds of things and then you will not want to be religious."

☞ FOR WORRIERS:
If you want others to have a sense of self-worth, tell them often: "That was a good decision. I knew I could trust you. I trust that you have the inner resources to deal with the obstacles in your life."

TAKE HEART!

After reading this list, you may feel discouraged. You may think, "I might just as well be silent for the rest of my life!" You may feel that life is filled with so much *ona'as devarim* that it is useless to even try and fight against it. You may also now be more aware of how abusive certain people act toward you, and may suddenly realize that trying to "forgive and forget" has only made this infectious virus worse. Or, you might feel terribly guilty, aware of all the people you have hurt in the past.

Take heart. Awareness is the first and most important step in growth. Simply being mindful of your own urge to engage in *ona'as devarim* will help you overcome it.

Don't be surprised if you complain to someone about others who are abusive and meet with a stone wall or find that you are blamed for provoking or deserving it, or are admonished and told, "Don't speak *lashon hara*."

Obviously, we need a revolution in consciousness. The Chafetz Chaim's classic work on *lashon hara* was considered revolutionary at the time he wrote it. Over the years, attitudes have changed. Now it's time for all of us to participate in a new revolution to eradicate *ona'as devarim*, this lesser-known aspect of forbidden speech.

How To Stay Loving
When Others Aren't

ONE

Identifying and Dealing with Unintentional Hurts

P eople will hurt us and we, inevitably, will hurt others, even if only unintentionally. When we feel hurt, the Torah tells us not to have hatred in our hearts, not to be vengeful or bear a grudge (Vayikra 19:17-18), but rather:

"LOVE YOUR FELLOWMAN AS YOURSELF"
· VAYIKRA 19:18 ·

This is easier said than done when someone has just disappointed us. Our minds may be burning with rage and our hearts broken with grief at the insults, disappointments and betrayals we experience. The only way to overcome disappointment is with faith:

"NO ONE HURTS HIS FINGER DOWN BELOW WITHOUT IT BEING DECREED ABOVE"
· CHULLIN 7B ·

In other words, there is a reason this is happening. It is a major test of our character. We can learn from the situation, about our strengths and weaknesses. The struggle to elevate ourselves spiritually in the midst of pain is not easy. The following tools will help.

REACTING TO HURT FROM PEOPLE WHO ARE USUALLY GOOD-HEARTED

When people with whom we usually have a positive relationship hurt our feelings, it is proper to immediately assume, "They did not intend to hurt." Nonetheless, we may choose to let the person know that we have been hurt, so that s/he will be more careful in the future. A spiritually refined person will express sincere regret for any pain caused, whereas insensitive people will attack, ridicule or deny that they did anything wrong.

It is not always easy to know which offenses to ignore and which to take seriously. With effort, you can become less judgmental and more forgiving of others.

However, what if people really are being tactless, bossy, inconsiderate, nosy, insensitive or even hateful? What can you do? The following suggestions can help you maintain your own *tzelem Elokim* (Godly image) even if others don't:

☞ STATE FEELINGS WITHOUT JUDGMENTS: Hostile thoughts are picked up by others subliminally and can wound as deeply as hostile words. So what can you do with your hurt feelings? Share the feelings in a way which does not hurt the other person. This means that you:

> ❧ Avoid judgments, such as: you are boring, childish, cruel, crazy, demanding, greedy, hysterical, inconsiderate, inept, insensitive, irresponsible, lazy, narrow-minded, petty, pushy, selfish, shallow, spoiled, stupid, untrustworthy, a total failure, etc. Even if the person has these negative traits, do not mention them! Judgments (spoken or unspoken) only make people feel nervous and hostile.

- Express your feeling by making "I" statements, thereby not condemning the other person: For example, say, "When you do that, I feel: anxious, stupid, ashamed, discouraged, undermined, helpless, hopeless, hurt, rejected, sad, threatened, unloved, unvalued, etc. Therefore, I ask you to __________."

- State your need: "For my sense of security, I would really appreciate it if you would/ would not..."

- Build a safe relationship by having many positive thoughts and expressing appreciative words to the person. A relationship is like a bank; every positive thought or word of appreciation is a deposit. Every criticism is a withdrawal.

- Avoid giving an entire laundry list of complaints at once (e.g., "You're not only lazy and selfish, you're also...").

- Do not dwell on the past. Do not play prosecuting attorney, bringing up numerous examples from the past to prove how horrible the person is.

- Let go of the consequences. Stating your feelings does not obligate the other person to comply. S/he may be unwilling or unable to give you want you want. Don't nag. Seek other options.

☞ PRAY: Ask Hashem to give you the strength to respond to rejection and disrespect in a respectful and civilized manner, i.e., with self-protective assertiveness, forgiveness, compassion and self-discipline.

When hurt, think to yourself:

> "This person is giving me the chance to put diffi-
> cult Torah principles into practice. I won't hold a
> grudge, hate or take vengeance, because then I
> corrupt my spirit with hatred. The more I prac-
> tice compassion, patience, forgiveness and love,
> the more I will feel Hashem's love." (Do not fol-
> low this advice with someone who has APD.)

> "This person is giving me the opportunity to de-
> velop an independent sense of self-worth. I de-
> fine my worth according to Hashem's standards,
> not human standards."

Pray for the person, that he have a complete recovery from
his insensitivity, tactlessness or even cruelty.

Do not get angry over anything that you cannot change.
If you can't change the situation, it means Hashem wants
it to be this way. This is when you must work on *hashlamah*
(accepting Hashem's will).

☞ GIVE PEOPLE THE BENEFIT OF THE DOUBT UNLESS THEY
ARE HABITUAL OFFENDERS: Unless someone is constantly
belittling and demeaning you, assume that those who
offend you have no intention of doing so. Tell yourself over
and over, until it becomes a firm conviction, "They're doing
the best they can with the level of awareness they have
right now."

Many people resist compassion because they think it
means ignoring their hurt feelings or excusing, justifying
or ignoring people's poor *middos!* In fact, judging others
favorably is merely the first step in the process of coping

with the problem in a rational manner. People need to know your limits and must be taught to respect them. Children, in particular, need clear rules and regulations. This must be done with respect, not rage and scorn.

You awaken compassion in your heart by thinking, "They're doing the best they can." Compassion frees you to think calmly about possible solutions. For example:

INNOCENT/UNAWARE:
"He doesn't even realize that I felt hurt by his remark or by his lack of attention to me."

INNOCENT/ACCIDENT:
"He really didn't mean to do it."

INNOCENT/IN PAIN:
"She is preoccupied with her own physical or emotional pain and cannot give me what I want."

INNOCENT/BAD MOOD:
"The person is simply in a bad mood. It has nothing to do with me!"

INNOCENT/EXERCISED POOR JUDGMENT:
"The person didn't realize that it was a poor decision at the time."

INNOCENT/FORGOT:
"He simply forgot to do what I wanted."

INNOCENT/TEMPORARY DYSFUNCTION:
"He is tired, hungry, worried, going through hormonal storms, coping with a loss."

INNOCENT/DELAYED:
"He must be late because of a traffic jam, bro-

ken watch or unexpected emergency. At any rate, I'm sure he has a good reason."

For frequent delays, perhaps,

"When she gets locked into an activity, she just can't stop."

INNOCENT/DIDN'T HEAR/SEE:
"He wasn't tuned into me. He was thinking of other things."

More frequent hurtful behavior:

INNOCENT/WRONGLY THINKS THAT CRITICISM IS HELPFUL OR EDUCATIONAL:
"This person truly believes that constant pressure and criticism is the only effective way to get people to improve."

INNOCENT/ATTACHMENT DISORDER:
"Due to abuse, s/he just doesn't know how to connect to people in a healthy way. S/he is very wounded emotionally."

INNOCENT/UNINTERESTED:
"S/he doesn't want a relationship with me. For the sake of my sanity, I will stop trying to get through."

INNOCENT/INSECURE:
"Like many people, when s/he feels insecure, s/he feels unloved and inadequate. When s/he lashes out, it's because subconsciously s/he wants to test if this gloomy assessment is true. The best thing is to provide reassurance by saying, "I love you. I have faith in your ability to

cope with this difficulty." [*Note*: In general, when men feel insecure, they do not want to talk until the mood passes. Afterwards, they want reassurance and appreciation. In general, when women feel down, they do want to talk it all out and be comforted and reassured of your love.]

INNOCENT/ATTENTION DEFICIT DISORDER:
"S/he has ADD, which makes makes it harder to get organized, control impulses, listen attentively, focus, remember and regulate emotions."

INNOCENT/HAS DIFFERENT SET OF BOUNDARIES:
"She thinks it's perfectly fine to walk into my bedroom and look into my closets."

"She thinks it's okay to ask questions about my private life and call at any hour of the day or night."

"This child thinks she has the right to tell me how to wash my dishes and discipline the younger children."

INNOCENT/THINKS IT'S LOVE:
"She thinks her criticism is helpful."

"He thinks he's being loving when he interrogates me about where I've been and who I've talked to and calls me ten times a day. He doesn't realize that he is alienating me with his possessiveness and jealousy."

INNOCENT/POOR CHEMISTRY:
"We have such different priorities/needs/ feelings/tastes/tempos, etc."

INNOCENT/ADDICTED:
"The person is in the grip of an addiction (to food, work, money, computers, etc.)."

INNOCENT/OBSESSIVE-COMPULSIVE DISORDER:
"Due to OCD, he gets hysterical if things are not spotless, in perfect order or done in the perfectly rigid, ritualized manner he has adopted."

INNOCENT/POOR *MIDDOS*:
"The person is simply not *atzil middos* [of refined character]. How sad."

INNOCENT/ONLY A CHILD:
"He hit back/made noise/made a mess/had a tantrum/drew on the walls/made demands — because that's what children sometimes do."

Always see children as innocent. Never think of small children as manipulative, as this is a sure-fire way to make yourself angry. Forgive children, especially under the age of seven, when true impulse control just begins. Do not ignore or justify misbehavior. Use misbehavior as an opportunity to educate, remind, suggest and direct with firmness but compassion.

INNOCENT/LEARNING-DISABLED:
Approximately 24% of all children have some learning disability. Many are too tense to sit still and concentrate. Criticizing, slapping, shaming or otherwise punishing them only increases their pain, when what they really need is extra compassion, and guidance.

INNOCENT/TESTING LIMITS:
"The child is expressing his individuality and desire for independence."

"He is testing to see how far he can go and what the limits are. He is testing to see if I'll stand firm, because he's insecure. Knowing that there are limits will help him feel safe."

INNOCENT/BORED:
"Children get crazy when bored. That's why the two-year-old took all the tissues out of the box, unrolled all the toilet paper and poured his cereal on the floor. There was no malicious intent! Children aren't criminals."

"Children need attention just like flowers need water. They are not bad for wanting attention. It is a natural need. I will encourage independence and creativity, but I do not want to crush their desire for connection altogether or the child will become damaged."

INNOCENT/A CRY FOR HELP:
"No child purposely breaks things, spills things, wets his bed, loses things or flunks tests in school. Even if it is deliberate, it is a cry for help."

After giving the benefit of the doubt, you can talk about your hurt feelings with a forgiving attitude.

The Chazon Ish expresses the art of forgiveness beautifully:

"A [highly evolved] person strives to do good to others. He greets everyone with a pleasant countenance. He worries lest he accidentally miss the mark and not give the other person precisely what his soul needs. He knows that hurting someone's honor is the greatest pain. Yet he himself never feels insulted, for the great love in his heart covers all sins. He prepares himself ahead of time with true love to ignore insults, for he realizes that most people are not *atzilei middos* [of refined character]" (*Emunah U-bitachon* pp. 13-14).

☞ IDENTIFY WHETHER OR NOT THE UNDERLYING MESSAGE IS TRUE: When you feel hurt, identify the message you think the person is trying to convey.

"You're stupid, crazy, selfish and lazy."

"You're unimportant and insignificant."

"You're irresponsible, unreliable and untrustworthy."

"You're unspiritual."

Now, ask yourself, "Is it true that I am the horrible things this person thinks?" By identifying the underlying message, you can decide whether you want to adopt that opinion or not.

Also ask: "Is it really true that the person is sending me this shame message? Or is it my own low self-esteem which makes me interpret his/her insensitivity and lack of good manners in an exaggerated manner?"

Also ask: "Have I perhaps been so demanding that the person just couldn't take it any more? Perhaps I provoked them?"

What if you think the condemnations are true and that you really are dumb, lazy or crazy? This is more problematic.

ᔆ *"From the time I was little, I felt that my father was deeply disappointed in me. I wasn't the brilliant scholar he wanted for a son. I felt he was right: I was garbage. This led to years of severe depression later on. Whenever I'm around people, I immediately think that they see me as my father did. So I'm awkward and self-conscious and tend to see everyone as deliberately attempting to hurt me."*

The most effective way to change a negative self-image is to consistently write down the times when you display good *middos*, i.e., when you make good decisions, are loving, disciplined, considerate, courageous and responsible (see Appendices).

☞ DEPERSONALIZE: Do you tend to think that every minor offense is deliberate and abusive? Do you get enraged if someone yawns when you talk, doesn't return a favor, forgets to call back, leaves a mess or disagrees with you? Do you furiously attack people who have accidentally hurt your feelings, and hold a grudge long after they have expressed remorse?

In most cases, this response is formed during childhood, when you were repeatedly hurt by the people you turned to for love. To change this pattern, make a conscious effort to depersonalize by saying, "I don't know what is in anyone's heart or mind."

Start with strangers, because with them, you usually don't have expectations or think you know their motives. For example, tell yourself, "The clerk isn't nasty just because of who I am. She's having a hard day." Keep reminding yourself, "People aren't out to get me. They are doing the best they can with the tools they have, and sometimes their lack of tools inadvertently causes me pain."

After mastering the art of depersonalization and forgiveness with strangers, try it on family members. For example:

A CHILD WON'T COOPERATE:
Old Thinking:
"This child is purposely trying to drive me crazy because he hates me. He's bad. He makes me feel like a failure. I'll hit him until he behaves properly."

New Thinking:
"He just has a bad habit. I will keep a notebook and write down his good deeds to remind me to see him in a positive light and to help me stay loving. *Middos* work is like orthodontics. It takes time to correct bad habits and teach him civilized behavior. During calm moments, I'll teach him how to speak respectfully when he is upset."

THE HUSBAND IS IN AN UNCOMMUNICATIVE MOOD:
Old thinking:
"He doesn't care about anyone but himself. He makes me feel worthless. If he's grouchy to me, I'll be just as mean back."

New thinking:
"He's just stressed out. I'll be extra nice."

"I'll wait patiently until the mood passes and not bother him."

"He was never trained to communicate his feelings."

"I need to work on *hashlamah* (accepting Hashem's will) and being happy with the portion He gave me."

"My husband is loving me to the best of his ability right now."

THE WIFE FORGOT TO GO TO THE CLEANERS:
Old thinking:
"She doesn't really care."

"She's so lazy."

New thinking:
"She probably just forgot. She has so much on her mind."

"My priorities are not her priorities."

Of course, not every situation calls for a forgiving smile:

A relative criticizes every little thing you do: If you tell her that she hurt your feelings, she attacks you back. You feel ill around her, but if you don't call, she calls and yells at you for neglecting her.

Old thinking:
"How can I please her and get her to like me? I'm sure she likes me underneath it all."

New thinking:
"This is third degree abuse. I must break this neurotic habit of trying to get love from people who don't love me. I need friends and activities which build my confidence."

"I can feel very sorry for her — from a distance."

☞ SPEAK UP FIRMLY AND RESPECTFULLY: If, after trying to forgive, you still feel hurt, you must tell the person how you feel in order to save the relationship. If you keep swallowing your pain in silent anguish, the relationship will grow cold and die. Or, the accumulated pain may cause you to explode in times of stress and others will have no idea why you are reacting in a way which seems so "inappropriate" to them. You may also develop physical symptoms from suppressing your feelings.

So speak up! But do so respectfully so that you will not be guilty of *ona'as devarim*. (This is especially true when speaking to one's parents. They are in a category by themselves.)

A very helpful response is to compassionately tell an angry person, "You must be in a lot of pain. Please tell me about it." Or, "I love you. Let's work this out together." A basically healthy person will usually calm down because of your compassion and will express his feelings. However, a person with APD sees kindness as weakness and will use your openness as an invitation to attack you even more.

If you were abused as a child, you may think, "I have no right to demand respect because I'm inferior to everyone else." If so, you need help to change your thinking and believe that, as a Godly being, you deserve respect as you are right now. In time, the truth will be internalized.

Although the following techniques will be very effective with some people and with some situations, they will be totally ineffective with others! The effort is in your hands; the results are up to Hashem!

WRITE A LETTER:
If appropriate, write to the person and share your feelings. Give some practical suggestions and convey your hope for future change. If appropriate, reassure him/her of your love. If the person is mentally disturbed, do not send the letter. However, it is very helpful to write a letter back to yourself, imagining what that person would say if s/he could value you and love you as you are. This is very healing!

SEEK A THIRD PERSON:
"We must consult with a Rav or therapist. We are only going in circles by ourselves."

GIVE INARTICULATE PEOPLE WORDS:
"Instead of slamming doors and getting cold, just tell me, 'I need quiet time by myself,' and I will respect your needs."

"What I need to hear you say is, 'You make good decisions. You're a good person. I like you.'"

STATE RULES:
"I don't allow *ona'as devarim* in this house."

"I really want to listen, but I have a principle that I do not respond when people over the age of two speak to me angrily. So please state your request again, and this time do it in a respectful tone of voice."

GIVE AN "I" STATEMENT:
"Although I'm sure you didn't mean to hurt me, your comment was very painful. When you _____ (e.g., talk that way), it makes me feel _____ (unloved)."

"I therefore suggest that you_____."

TEST FOR CONCERN ON THE
PART OF THE OTHER PERSON:
"I am very hurt by what you did. May I tell you why?"

If the person is not interested, feel the grief and look elsewhere for love.

To an Advice Giver, Ask
For Reflective Listening:

"I know you like to find solutions, but I need to share my feelings without you giving me advice. Please just listen and sympathize."

"For the sake of my self-confidence and self-respect I need to make my own decisions."

"I appreciate your desire to help, but it makes me feel inferior. I want a relationship of equality."

To an Anti-Emotional Type,
Assert Your Right to Feel What You Feel:

"It might not hurt you, but it hurts me. This is my personal truth. Pain is very personal and subjective. The fact that you aren't pained by this does not make you superior."

To an Arguer, Disregard the Negative
Message, But Thank the Person
For Information:

"You have a point. Thank you for the information."

"Whenever we talk about this subject, we get into an argument. Our relationship is too important to me to let this happen, so let's agree not to discuss this subject."

To a Complainer:

"Do you want to just vent your anger, or do you want to find a solution to the problem?"

To a Dependent Type:

"You are welcome to call/visit only during the following hours."

TO A DEMANDING TYPE:
"That's a want, not a need. I have time for needs, but not always for wants."

You might tell the person that you feel stifled, for:

"WHEN DEMANDS BEGIN, LOVE DEPARTS"
• STRIVE FOR TRUTH!,* VOL. 1, P. 132 •

"I have full faith in your ability to handle this on your own. You make good decisions."

TO AN INTERROGATOR:
"I'm curious as to why you said/did that. Please explain why you said/did that."

"Why do you want to know?" (Always respond to their questions with questions.)

TO A NAME-CALLER:
"For the sake of our relationship, I demand an apology. You are not allowed to speak to me like that."

TO A NIT-PICKER:
"I focus my energies only on those things that have eternal value for me. If I got upset about every little thing, I'd have no time left for what is really important."

"I love you. But your criticism is destroying my sense of self-worth and my desire to be around you. Just as people eat three meals a day, they need three compliments a day to stay healthy.

---

* Rabbi Eliyahu E. Dessler, trans. by Rabbi Aryeh Carmell, Feldheim Publishers.

You can start now."

To a possessive type, assert your need to do things that bring you joy:
"This activity is like oxygen for me. It makes me feel alive. If you stop me, my spirit will die."

To a perfectionist:
"I don't have a scrubbing gene."

"I will do my best to keep things neat and orderly, but I will not waste my life scrubbing, dusting or shining things."

Remind them, "There is no man so wholly righteous on earth that he always does good and never sins" (*Koheles* 7:20). Perfectionists have a need to feel superior; praising them may give them what they need to hear.

ଔ *"When my mother lived with us, she criticized everything I did, including how I fed and dressed the children. She told them not to listen to me when I disciplined them. I felt it was disrespectful to tell her how hurt I felt, so I swallowed the pain while my life became a living hell. It was only when I was hospitalized with a bleeding ulcer that I finally went to a Rav who told me that it was necessary to find other accommodations for her. I might have saved the relationship if I had set boundaries sooner. My husband, too, realizes that if he had defended me, things would not have gotten so out of hand."*

ଔ *"I was always the type to do anything for shalom bayis. Because of my not standing up for my honor as a mother, people looked down on me. Even though my own daughter was very nasty to me, I swallowed my pain for the sake of the grand-children and because I was so lonely. I suffered from her for years until I finally got the courage to say, 'I will not visit unless you speak to me with respect.' For three painful weeks, she did not call. Finally, she apologized. Since then, she is careful about how she talks to me. I wish I had spoken up earlier."*

You may think that the only way to preserve a relationship is by swallowing your pain. But relationships die when there is no communication. Don't think you lost a relationship by being honest — you lost only an illusion of a relation-ship.

☞ USE YOUR IMAGINATION TO PREPARE YOURSELF: Save yourself from a future outburst by visualizing possible situ-ations in which your feelings might get hurt, and by seeing yourself responding in a firm tone, convinced of your right to be treated with respect.

You can also use your imagination to let go of non-nur-turing people. Mentally send them off in a hot-air balloon or rocket ship to Hashem. Each time you think of someone with whom you cannot communicate, repeat this tactic. You can also prepare yourself for true rebuke by realizing that a person on a high spiritual level is happy that his best friend rebukes him honestly, because:

> a. It brings him joy to know that his friend loves him enough to be honest and point out a fault. [*Note*: This works only if the one rebuked feels truly loved and if the rebuke is occasional and not scornful.]

> b. It gives him the opportunity to work on him-self and improve if the rebuke is correct.

c. If the person is incorrect, then the insult gives him the opportunity for a major spiritual victory, for,

"THOSE HUMILIATED WHO DO NOT HUMILIATE IN TURN,
WHO HEAR THEIR INSULT AND DO NOT RETORT, WHO DO
EVERYTHING OUT OF LOVE AND REJOICE IN THEIR OWN
AFFLICTION ARE LIKE THE SUN BURSTING FORTH
IN ALL ITS GLORY"
• SHABBOS 88B •

However, it is impossible to remain unaffected by constant criticism from a person with whom one lives or works, especially if one is dependent on this person physically, emotionally or financially.

☞ FORMULATE YOUR OWN "SANITY RULES" AND TELL OTH-ERS WHAT THEY ARE: You may think you cannot be assertive about *ona'as devarim*. However, you have no trouble telling someone, "I don't allow pork in my home." Once you realize how toxic *ona'as devarim* is, you can let others know:

"I will not allow any *ona'as devarim* in this house."

"Cleanliness is definitely important to me. But my priority in life is people, not things."

"I do not want to agonize over this issue. I want to focus on solutions."

"If it's not forbidden by the Torah, then it's not a sin!"

"I don't speak when I'm hostile, because I don't want to hurt anyone. Instead, I read *Tehillim* until I feel calm and loving."

"When I feel hostile, I either remove myself from the company of people or, if I can, ask for their love and reassurance."

"When people are upset, we give them more love."

☞ DO NOT FEAR HONESTY: Emotionally healthy people respect you more when you are honest. So let others know:

"I like when you do X, but I don't like when you do Y."

"I cannot speak to you between 5:00 and 8:00. That is when I'm helping the children with their homework and putting them to bed. They are my first priority."

"Please call before coming to visit."

"I'd really like to help, but I can't right now."

"No, I can't do that. It makes me uncomfortable."

"I don't make fancy meals. Simple is fine with me." (Same for fancy clothes.)

While honesty may be wonderful, it has its limits. Communication is not a magic formula which solves all problems. Simply telling someone you don't like their behavior is no guarantee that they will change. People may be incapable of giving you what you want. Those who dislike you for being honest are not the kind of people you want as friends.

☞ DO NOT ENGAGE IN INTERCHANGES WITH PEOPLE WHO ARE IN A BAD MOOD: When people are hostile, hateful, hurting (or hungry) it is usually useless to try to reason with them. In fact, doing so may make them angrier. Wait until their mood improves. Then talk. If you cannot separate from someone who is often hostile and who uses the information you share to attack you later, this is a very great tragedy, akin to being sentenced to a harsh prison camp where beatings are frequent. All you can do is strengthen your faith in the midst of the pain.

As children, we usually feel compelled to respond to everything that happens in the external world. As adults, we can learn not to respond, when not responding is the more rational and effective choice. It's a choice we must make very often.

☞ DEFEND YOUR FAMILY MEMBERS: If you have a critical in-law, make sure your husband stands up for you. If he does not do so, your marriage and your mental health will be endangered. Wives should do the same if their husbands are suffering put-downs from anyone in their family. Parents should also stand up for their children and not allow verbally abusive teachers or principals to victimize them.

☞ TEACH CHILDREN TO SPEAK RESPECTFULLY WHEN THEY ARE UPSET: Many people think that they have the right to hurt others back when they feel hurt. Prove to your children that they need not give in to this impulse. Tell them, "See, I'm upset with you, but I'm not screaming or hitting. I'm practicing self-control. We must all work on this *middah*. That's what maturity is all about."

If two children are fighting, call time out and separate them until they can speak respectfully. During calm times, have practice sessions where you show them how to work out arguments in a respectful way. For example, say, "Let's say you both want to play with the computer at the same time. Here's a cup with numbered pieces of paper inside. Whoever picks the highest number gets to play with it first."

Encourage children to express their feelings and help them find the right words. Don't allow them to interrupt when the other one is speaking. Children enjoy this game and when they see how important speaking respectfully is to you, they will want to speak that way more often.

Be empathetic toward children when they express pain. Then they will be more compassionate toward you.

The loose-leaf binder technique is the best miracle tool of all (see Appendices). Ask children once or twice a day, "Tell me when you have restrained a harmful impulse." Then write it down in a special notebook. You can even give a prize when the child reaches a certain number of victories. Children quickly learn that behavior they thought was not controllable can in fact be controlled.

Read off your own and their major victories at the Shabbos table and cheer everyone!

☞ REBUKE WITH LOVE: Many justify verbal abuse by calling it "constructive criticism." This is like a criminal calling a stabbing "corrective surgery." Don't confuse a stabbing with surgery. Do not perform surgery on people who don't want it. You may protest, "I'm only trying to help," but your rebuke will do damage unless the recipient is truly receptive and you are truly respectful. To rebuke properly, follow the following rules (based on *Hilchos De'os* 6:7):

ೞ Feel respect for the other person. Don't even

think of opening your mouth if you are feeling hostile. Be honest! Your anger alerts you to the fact that you need to take the time to accept Hashem's will and have compassion for others.

ᙇ Be sure the person being rebuked knows and feels this love at the time of the rebuke. For example:

"That's not fitting for a fine person like you."

"I'm worried about you. Research shows that anger raises the cholesterol level, making people more prone to heart attacks. Because I care, I hope you can work this out without anger."

ᙇ Speak in a low tone of voice.

ᙇ Speak in private. (Teachers, take note!)

ᙇ Only mention a trait which you know the person is capable of changing. It is no use rebuking a person for something which is part of his very nature (e.g., don't rebuke someone for being intellectual, emotional, shy, meticulous, hyperactive, etc.).

ᙇ Rebuke the other person for his own benefit, to remind him of his tzelem Elokim, not out of a need to change or dominate.

ᙇ Have a solution in mind when possible. For example:

ADULT CHILD TO PARENT:
"Since the children's behavior upsets you, how

about visiting after they're asleep?"

TO LEARNING-DISABLED CHILD:
"Since it's sometimes difficult to concentrate, I'll provide a study space which is free of distractions."

"Taking medication will help you focus. This is no more shameful than wearing glasses."

TO UNCOOPERATIVE CHILD:
"In this home, we all share responsibilities. Here is a list of chores. Which three would you like to do? I made a chart. You can put a check by the ones you do each day."

TO HABITUAL LATE-COMER:
In a non-judgmental tone of voice, say,

"For my peace of mind, I like to arrive on time. So I'll go by myself and we'll meet there."

TO SPOUSE WITH SHOPPING ADDICTION:
"We have an appointment with a financial advisor who will help us make a budget."

TO PROCRASTINATOR:
"Since we both tend to put things off, let's build each other up by celebrating when we do manage to make the doctors' appointments we need and actually keep them."

"Let's agree on a deadline, and if it's not done by then, I'll take care of it myself."

"I get frantic when things are done at the last minute. So, for my sense of emotional stability, please let me take care of this myself."

☞ USE POSITIVE REINFORCEMENT: *Middos* improvement requires constant effort. To encourage growth, "reward" others by writing a note of thanks or praise when they make any small attempts to improve their *middos*. If you are always sighing with disappointment, grumbling under your breath or shaming them, you will not only be indulging in *ona'as devarim*, you'll be reinforcing their negative behavior!

The best way to encourage improvement is to look for the good — no matter how rare it may be — and say how happy it makes you to see that behavior. For example:

STINGY SPOUSE:
When the person does give in any way, no matter how minor, enthusiastically endorse him/her. When one woman's husband made a large donation to charity, she had the letter of thanks that he received framed to honor him. This encouraged him to give more often.

UNCOMMUNICATIVE CHILD:
When the child does talk, even for a few seconds, tell him how much better you felt, even if this is stretching the truth a bit.

MESSY SPOUSE:
Look for any area that is neat. Then endorse enthusiastically. Help the person clean. Many people suffer from poor organizational skills.

DEMANDING SPOUSE:
Let her know how much you appreciate it when she leaves you alone and show enthusiasm when she pursues her own hobbies and interests.

Even with all your efforts, however, people may not improve. Whether they do or not is in their hands, not yours. Most people must learn to live with a certain level of disappointment in their family members. Trying to change people who don't want to change will do nothing but turn you into a nasty nag.

Take assertive action if your sanity is threatened. For example, you may need to send a hostile child to a dormitory, or get a job so that you spend less time around a hostile spouse.

☞ TEACH PEOPLE EMPATHY: Using a ruler, tell people that when anyone's pain level is over "6," they should just empathize, in keeping with the principle, "Do not comfort a person in the hour when his dead lies before him" (*Pirkei Avos* 4:18). Our Sages also say that "bearing the burden with another" (*Pirkei Avos* 6:6) means sharing his pain. Simply being with the person is one way of showing love. This means no advising, philosophizing, moralizing or judging. Just listen.

☞ FORGIVE FOR NO REASON OTHER THAN TO BECOME A MORE LOVING PERSON. We say each night:

"Master of the Universe, I hereby forgive anyone who has angered or vexed me, or sinned against me, either physically or financially, against my honor or anything else that is mine, whether accidentally or intentionally by speech or by deed..."

Forgiveness is not meant to lead to passivity or self-deception. We are not supposed to forgive those who are truly evil. As for those who have emotional disturbances, we may not feel forgiving at the moment they are hurting us. But it is a goal to strive for later on.

If Hashem said to forgive, it must be for our good. And it must be that we are capable of doing so. Holding on to resentments is like holding hot coals — we will only get burned. Resentment ties up energy which could be invested in loving those who can appreciate our love and engaging in activities which benefit the world, such as charity projects, learning Torah or learning new skills.

If you are not getting sufficient love from others, learn positive ways to cope with the pain. Get busy with fulfilling activities. Go out and exercise vigorously when you feel like exploding; it's a good way to get rid of toxic emotions.

Forgiveness is the natural result of *emunah*, trusting that the events and people Hashem sends to us are precisely what we need to reveal our spiritual greatness.

Unless a person is actively abusive, do not allow your level of compassion or love be determined by their actions. Love others without demands, not only for your own health and sanity, but because this is what God wants.

TWO

IDENTIFYING
AND DEALING
WITH CHRONIC
OFFENDERS

D o you feel confused, stupid, ashamed or discouraged around a certain person? If so, you may be dealing with someone who is more than merely insensitive. The person may be suffering from (APD) Abusive Personality Disorder. In such a case, nothing you do will ever satisfy them. They use criticism or other offensive tactics to keep you at a distance, because closeness is threatening to them.

Dealing with disturbed people requires a different set of rules from those that you use around normal people. With most people, giving the benefit of the doubt, overlooking faults and focusing on the good is often the best tactic. You do your utmost to make peace and avoid arguments. You can usually resolve problems by talking about them. Normal people respond to love and positive reinforcement.

But being honest and expressing feelings to people with APD often backfires. The more you overlook and minimize, the worse the "infection" becomes. They are extremely suspicious and misinterpret your attempts at frank discussion as a personal attack. The slightest hint that they are imperfect or that you do not accept their domination gives them cause to attack you. People with aps are often so unreasonable and their responses so bizarre and vicious that talking only makes you feel crazier.

One of the worst results of living with an emotionally disturbed person is that the healthy partner also begins to deteriorate. Many basically happy, affectionate people become nasty and cold in order to provide themselves with some sense of protection. The loss of a positive sense of self is one of the major losses in such a situation.

Nothing hurts more than pain which cannot be expressed. This is a pain with which many live, much like those who live with a chronic illness which causes excruciating pain. The difference is that a person living with unexpressed pain cannot speak about it for fear of being labeled a failure or being accused of speaking *lashon hara*.

Defining APD is difficult, since no one is abusive all the time. Even the most hostile person can act friendly at times. Thus, any label, such as "APD," is likely to be questioned by someone who has had a different experience with that person. During good times, you too may doubt your own conclusions and wonder if perhaps you're exaggerating or not seeing the truth.

It is to the abuser's advantage to be inconsistent and keep the victims off-balance, unsure of themselves and feeling slightly (or very!) inferior and crazy. This way, s/he can a) control them; b) justify the abuse; and c) come out "smelling like a rose" in the public's eye for putting up with such "crazy" people.

Learn to protect yourself in the following ways:

Recognize the signs of APD: You wouldn't choose to drive through a war zone. When you see any of the following warning signs, make a detour:

A carefully constructed facade of normality and morality presented to the outside world

alternating with episodes of cursing, immorality and explosive rage and cruelty in private:
One of the hallmarks of APD is inconsistency. People with APD are often quite charming in public and well thought of by outsiders, in contrast to their behavior in private. Even at home, they can be nice one minute and cruel the next. They might give generously to a charity, but be extremely stingy to family members. They can be abusive to one family member but extra nice to others, or nice to the grandchildren but nasty to their own children. Thus, victims are kept in a state of confusion, sure that, "If they can be so nice, I must be the bad one or I'd be treated nicely too." "I must be crazy since my version of what happened is totally different from theirs."

Many abusive people are often gracious hosts, helpful to outsiders and active in community affairs. This is because the symptoms of emotional disturbance tend to be worse among close family members. Outsiders refuse to believe that such "nice," very normal people are capable of being so stingy, explosive and abusive in private and often scorn the victim who complains as a liar or exaggerator.

Pathological lying:
People with APD twist facts and lie with a smile. They have no inner integrity. They change personalities as others change clothing.

The compulsion to always be right and superior is very destructive in human relationships. It causes them to attack anyone who even hints that they may be imperfect or may have made a mistake. Telling someone with APD, "You've hurt my feelings," implies that s/he is imperfect, which sets off a flurry of accusations and distortions.

Lack of remorse or pity:

They have no pity for those who suffer from their attacks nor do they feel guilt when they are apprised of their cruelty. In fact, they do not think they have done anything wrong. They are indifferent and oblivious to the pain they cause others. Instead, they see themselves as righteous and demand that the victim see himself as guilty.

Excessive pride and haughtiness:
They have a distorted perception of themselves. They see themselves as superior (if not downright saintly!) and view everyone else as inferior.

Contempt for others expressed in scorn, ridicule and sarcasm:
They view any display of emotion as a sign of immaturity, stupidity or insanity, though they themselves may be very hot-tempered.

Lack of self-awareness:
They are oblivious to their own faults and the pain they inflict on others, which is why attempts to drag them to therapy often fail.

Extreme jealousy and possessiveness
They interrogate you about every aspect of your life in a suspicious manner.

Blaming others for their own mistakes
They deny responsibility for their problems, holding others responsible.

Excessive attention to petty external details
They will often comment about your dress, speech and behavior, seeking any excuse to make you feel inferior.

Use of force to solve conflicts:
They must have their way immediately.

DO NOT CONFUSE ABUSE WITH "LOVE": Normal human beings have such a strong need for love that they often imagine that an abuser is loving even though they are hurt over and over by that person. They are further confused if the person insists, "I love you. I'm only criticizing you to help you." In addition, well-meaning outsiders often whitewash the abuse by saying: "S/he really loves you underneath it all/isn't really abusive/ isn't responsible for his actions/was provoked/is insecure and needs you to be submissive to boost his fragile ego."

Thus, the victim's illusion of power ("If I just tried harder...") is matched by the illusion of love that the abuser tries to present when cornered ("I didn't mean it. No one is as caring as I am").

Although every person has his dark moments, a loving person is consistently loving and feels bad if he accidentally hurts someone. A loving person encourages those around him to fulfill their potential to the fullest. A loving person does not crush others with constant criticism. While abusers believe they are truly loving people if they occasionally buy a gift or do a chore, this is not love. People who love will consistently:

> ❧ Take time to listen to your feelings without making you feel bad.

> ❧ Take the time to show interest in what interests you.

> ❧ Love you just the way you are, even though you probably have some faults and peculiarities.

> ❧ Encourage you to be all you can be, to develop your talents to the fullest, to do what you love

and what brings you joy.

It is part of a spouse's job to make you feel cherished. Calling abuse love will make you feel crazy.

If you are told to respect or love someone who is abusing you, this forces you to lie. When you invalidate your feelings and deny your reality, this damages your sense of integrity and identity.

DO NOT BLAME YOURSELF FOR THE BAD *MIDDOS* OF THE ABUSER: People with APD have two main strategies: a) "Katyusha rocket attacks," in which they humiliate their victims directly with words of contempt; and b) "faulty Chernobyl reactors," which silently radiate a steady leak of poisonous hostility. They will blame you (or their parents, your parents, neighbors, siblings, allergies, hormones, etc.) for their hostility. Don't fall into the blame trap. Adopt a new way of thinking:

> *Old Thinking:*
> "If he's angry, I must have done something wrong to provoke it. I must be too demanding or dumb. If I just knew how to communicate, I would be able to get through to him/her. I must not be trying hard enough."

> *New Thinking:*
> "I deserve to be treated with respect even if I am imperfect and haven't satisfied all his/her needs. Nothing justifies disrespect or cruelty."

> *Old Thinking:*
> "If she treats me as though I'm inferior, it must mean that I really am inferior."

> "It's all my fault that I am not liked."

New Thinking:
"Just because s/he acts superior does not mean s/he is superior! I'm a success in Hashem's eyes for all the effort I put forth to be a refined human being."

Old Thinking:
"It's all up to the woman. I can change him if I just try hard enough."

New Thinking:
"I think there are doors, when, in truth, maybe this is a wall. I cannot remain loving when I am being constantly mocked and rejected."

"People's *middos* are their own responsibility, not mine." (Of course, parents are responsible to help their children develop good *middos*.)

Old Thinking:
"If I were perfect, things would be calm. After all, s/he's so nice to others. So it must be my fault."

New Thinking:
"S/he has an illness which manifests itself as a compulsion to punish, belittle and control me. People with APD will always find some reason to hurt others. It's not my fault. For the sake of my sanity, I must detach myself from him/her."

PRACTICE THE ART OF REFINED SILENCE:

"DO NOT ANSWER A FOOL — LEST YOU BECOME LIKE HIM"
• MISHLEI 26:4 •

Advisors say, "Keep talking," but communication is impossible when you try to express your feelings and the other person says:

> "I don't know what you're talking about. I never hurt you. You're imagining things."

> "There are institutions for people who get so emotional."

> "Everyone else thinks I'm a saint."

The Rambam recommends silence toward those who are mentally defective (*Hilchos De'os* 6:9). So what do you do with the pain? One possibility is to talk to God:

> "Hashem, I know You will reward me for staying civilized even when others aren't, because it is so very difficult to control myself when I am 'overfilled with the derision of the complacent and the scorn of the arrogant' (*Tehillim* 122). Help me to elevate myself by not answering back and by overcoming my urge to be cruel in return. Help me retain my sense of dignity in the midst of indignity. Let me feel Your love so that I will not feel so alone, unloved and unloveable."

> "Hashem, help me to disconnect from this person, so that I am not constantly being hurt."

> "Hashem, thank you for giving me this opportunity to improve my *middos*, to practice silence, self-protection, assertiveness, etc."

> "Hashem, I make Your will my will. Only You can give me the strength to go on and protect my spirit from harm."

"Hashem, I trust that the angels are up there dancing and cheering because I didn't return an insult with an insult." (Some offenders are stunned into silence when this is said out loud! Others use it as another excuse to mock you.)

"Hashem, I was created in Your image. You alone determine my worth, not human beings. I value myself as You made me. I deserve to be cherished as I am. If You have kept me alive, I must have something of value to contribute to the world, if only my love for You and my loving smile to those who can appreciate me."

DISCONNECT: Rabbi Simcha Zissel, the Alter from Kelm, wrote, "I want to associate only with people whom I recognize to be *nosei b'ol*." It was the single criterion which qualified a student for admission into his yeshivah (*Chochmah U-mussar* 1:10).

Within certain limits, you have the same right to choose the people with whom to associate. If you get upsetting physical symptoms or feel you are losing your mind around a certain person, you may have no choice but to disconnect.

How can you test if a person is merely insensitive or truly abusive? One possibility is to state your feelings, such as, "I'm sure you didn't mean to offend me, but you hurt my feelings." An emotionally healthy person will usually apologize quickly or within a few days.

However, if the person becomes sarcastic or says you deserve to be hurt, face reality. You might need to say, "Please do not phone or visit unless you can speak respectfully to me." Taking such a stand is not easy, but it is the only way to initiate change. You may feel like a bad person and be tempted to appease and do anything to win them back, especially if he calls you names, threatens you or sends a third party to make you feel guilty for not making peace, i.e., giving in to all his demands. Be aware that any "peace conference" is likely to be one in which you are pressured to make all the concessions. Be aware that the person will probably say s/he has no idea why you are upset, yet when you try to explain yourself, you are attacked again. If the person does not apologize, remain distant. Do not initiate contact. Give him time to regret his actions. After a period of time has passed, the person may apologize and be more respectful.

    cs *"I invited a few relatives for my son's birthday party. As usual, they sat around attacking me and my way of life. For the first time, I stood up and said, 'Enough! This is sinas chinam. This is why the Beis Ha-mikdash was destroyed! I won't have it in my home. All people deserve to be treated with dignity, me included.' Since then, they visit less frequently. When they do, things are a little cold, but at least they don't attack me directly."*

Obviously, this does not work for a spouse, unless you have a place to go and are not in danger of being accused of abandonment. You cannot speak to an abusive parent in this way, but you can minimize contact or even move away to protect your sanity.

Breaking off a relationship with a relative is very difficult. Even if you do not speak to them directly, their hostile accusations may continue to ring in your head for years. You may constantly blame yourself for not having tried harder or for being too sensitive and obsess about what more you might have done or said — might do or say in the future — to just get through and make them understand. You may need the help of a therapist to deal with this trauma.

TAKE RESPONSIBILITY AND BE ASSERTIVE WHEN POSSIBLE: Many people think, "I should be able to take the insults. I shouldn't be so sensitive." Wrong! You cannot be unaffected by abuse. Abusers are only stopped when others take tough action. Start small to build up your courage. Try the following:

ca End prolonged phone conversations which upset you.

ca Say, "I prefer not to talk about this issue."

ca Get the name of abusive salespersons, taxi drivers, doctors, nurses, bus drivers, repairmen, etc. Write a letter to their supervisor.

DON'T LISTEN TO THOSE WHO SAY, "SOMETHING MUST BE WRONG WITH YOU. IF YOU WANTED TO STOP THE ABUSE, YOU WOULD." This is like accusing the Jews of cowardice or masochism during the Holocaust. If a victim remains silent it is usually because of fear. Abusers are often in positions of power and will crush anyone who challenges their authority. It's the abuser who has the machine gun. Confrontation is likely to bring swift retaliation. For example:

ca After a parent complains about classroom abuse, a teacher may refuse to call on the child for the rest of the school year, may ridicule him frequently in class or give him extra homework or other punishments.

ca A child might be expelled from school.

ca A worker who complains about abuse may be

fired from his job and then ruined financially by lawsuits.

ଔ A wife who speaks up may be deprived of grocery money and other basic necessities or even beaten, if not worse.

ଔ An adult child may be disowned.

ଔ The husband may be accused of being a molester, may have his reputation ruined and be ruined financially if the abusive wife has rich family members who hire powerful lawyers who don't mind lying.

ଔ Police may take action against the one who files a complaint when the abuser invents stories accusing the victim of being abusive.

If you have been "sentenced" to a period of time with such a person, do not expect to manage easily. It is very difficult to maintain your sanity when someone is constantly telling you that you are stupid or crazy and do not deserve to be loved or respected.

THREE

IF YOU ARE MARRIED TO SOMEONE WITH APD

Abusers rarely marry other abusers. They usually marry good-hearted types who go to extraordinary lengths to keep the marriage together. Victims tend to be unusually responsible, self-sacrificing and devoted. Despite the pain and terror they live with, most hold down jobs and have good relationships with non-abusive people. If anything, they are too forgiving, bearing their pain in stoic silence until the situation becomes truly unbearable.

There is nothing more painful than to be rejected by a close family member. It is even more difficult if that person is often scornful and enraged, then suddenly warm and affectionate, or demeaning yet demanding of affection. Marriage to a hostile person is a tragedy no one could foresee, since attachment disorders usually manifest themselves only after marriage. If this has happened to you:

❑ TAKE ACTION EARLY IN THE RELATIONSHIP, before the pattern of abuse has been established. Do not dismiss scorn, sarcasm and mockery, especially in the beginning of a marriage. It must be clear from the outset: no "ona'as devarim" in this house! Fatigue, stress, hunger and bad moods are not excuses to belittle, explode, throw things or curse. If you make concession after concession, the person learns that you will tolerate abuse and it will escalate.

However, truly abusive people have no concern for others' feelings. They will accuse you of being critical for pointing out that they are critical. There is little you can do with someone who has no conscience to appeal to. And since such people think of themselves as the only higher authority worthy of respect, they usually refuse all outside help.

Although some people will cry "abuse" at the drop of a hat, most victims are too forgiving and keep their marriage together at all costs. No normal person wants to get divorced, with all the pain and trauma involved. Most think, "If I just work harder on the relationship, am more accepting and optimistic, things are certain to improve."

At first, the healthy spouse bounces back from the attacks and even prides him/herself on being so forgiving. But it is impossible to build a healthy marriage with someone who lies, uses force against you and explodes whenever his/her demands are not met.

Get help immediately if you even suspect that your spouse has APD. Do not shrug off repeated violent episodes as "flukes." Do not return to an advisor who tells you, "Don't pay any attention to it. Grow some "elephant skin...." You will not get elephant skin; you will get PTSD (Post-Traumatic Stress Disorder — see p.193). Eventually, your love will turn to disgust or indifference. This is the final stage, which signals that an emotional divorce has taken place internally, even if you never divorce officially.

Ongoing therapy is required to help a person overcome abusive tendencies. You might say, "The condition for my remaining with you is that you see a therapist." Be prepared to follow through! Also be prepared to hear your spouse tell you that you are the crazy one who needs a therapist.

People with APD rarely go to therapy. They usually claim

that psychology is nonsense. If they do go, under pressure, they go once and then say that it did not work. Those who do go to a therapist often spend the time justifying themselves and accusing others of being abusive to them and not appreciating how loving they are. They may provide a list of items they have purchased, as if material gifts prove their love.

Many disturbed people become more enraged if you try to enlist the support of another family member, a friend, your family physician, rabbi or social worker. [*Note:* If an abuser knows that you have seen a therapist, you may be accused of being insane in any future court case, so keep this fact hidden.]

❑ DO NOT HOPE FOR CHANGE FROM PEOPLE WHO DO NOT PUT EFFORT INTO CHANGING: You cannot heal another person. A person can improve any behavior, but only if he: a) is aware that he has a problem and b) makes an effort to improve. If a person doesn't think anything is wrong, he won't change. You cannot make someone change. Passive methods, such as slipping calming drops into their juice, won't help. Change requires conscious, repeated effort. Exaggerated hopefulness is perpetuated by:

a. INTERMITTENT CONDITIONING:

Just as ordinary people become hooked on gambling, people can become hooked on abusive relationships, sure that they will "win the jackpot" if they are just patient and persevere long enough. The inconsistency of people with APD makes it extremely difficult to break off relationships with them. You would avoid someone who was always angry. But because people with APD do provide occasional gifts, money, affection or help, you may be convinced that you can get more if you just try harder. This is called "intermittent conditioning." It is almost impossible to extinguish, for the gifts keep your false hopes alive. It's what makes people hope that they will actually win the lottery.

b. DON'T FALL INTO CO-DEPENDENCY:

"Co-dependency" is the term used to define a neurotic habit where an individual endlessly tries to change or control people who remain resistant to his attempts, or tries to win the love of people who continuously scorn and reject him. He will use any or all of the following behaviors, often for years on end: lecturing, begging, sulking, advising, bending over backwards to please, suffering years of abuse in stoic silence, raging, threatening, placating, provoking, trying to impress, dragging a person to counseling against his/her will, checking up on a person phoning, locking out/locking in, scolding, sighing constantly, punishing, etc. They give up their integrity, independence and identity in the hope of getting the love they so desperately seek. No matter how often these tactics fail, co-dependents are sure that the next conversation will bring success.

It is extremely difficult to break this pattern. Hope is a co-dependent's enemy; he must face the reality that his dreams cannot be fulfilled by this person. Only then can he move on and form healthier relationships based on mutual trust and respect.

Co-dependents keep thinking, "If I just persist long enough, I'll get what I want from this person." They must realize that they have an addiction, similar to that of an alcoholic. They must keep reminding themselves, "This person is like alcohol for me. Before I start, I'm sure I'll get satisfaction. But after each communication, I end up with the same old results: guilt, shame, confusion, and rage. If I really want my sanity, I must wean myself away from this relationship."

c. The Appearance of Change:

People can appear to change without making any real changes. Hope is kept alive with the "Bouquet of Flowers Ploy." After an attack, when you are feeling most hurt, perhaps contemplating divorce or suicide, the abuser brings a bouquet of flowers or some other gift and says, "I've changed! I've turned over a new leaf." Desperate to believe "s/he really does love me," you begin to hope. At this point, there is an illusion that you are the one with the power and that if you just make concessions, the "peace process" will succeed. If not, you are the "bad guy." So you try again. A honeymoon period follows. You think, "It's a whole new marriage." But slowly the machine gun comes out and the insults escalate. Feeling betrayed, you again contemplate divorce or suicide. In the depths of despair, you are again given some gift and the cycle of hope and despair begins anew. This can go on for years without anyone realizing that no real change has ever taken place.

❑ Do not tie your joy or self-worth to any human being: Ordinarily, our greatest happiness is derived from our close relationships. However, if you are married to an abuser, you must find other sources of joy and self-esteem. Abusers try to keep you blind to the truth that you have a Godly essence. They try to move you off-center with contempt, because this is the fastest way to gain control over you.

ଔ *"The hardest thing about living with an abusive wife is that I started to hate myself. I hated what I turned into around her — mean, nervous and nasty. As a man, it is even more shameful to admit that I was abused. Who would believe that this charming woman could be so cold and ruthless? People aren't used to thinking of men as sensitive and vulnerable."*

Victor Frankl, a survivor of Auschwitz, said, "The only sane response to insanity is insanity." Instinctively, to protect yourself, you become cold, angry, silent or withdrawn. If you become numb, you are seen as uncaring. If you get angry, you are accused of being hysterical. If you go to a therapist, they accuse you of being crazy. If you are silent, it is assumed that everything is fine and that you have nothing to complain about. The sense of being trapped is devastating.

Abuse causes you to lose touch with your Godly center, to lose touch with what you love most about yourself — the loving, spontaneous, creative person you once were or seek to be. You must fight to stay sane, which means staying centered in the truth of your Godly essence.

Even if you feel broken, dress nicely. Make sure you exercise regularly. Watch your weight. Get a job. Open your own private bank account. Find creative outlets, such as music, writing and art. Do everything possible to maintain your sense of self-worth and your identity. Know that you have Godly value.

❑ TAKE A STAND WHENEVER POSSIBLE: At some point, you must set limits, at which time you will probably be accused of being selfish, mean and crazy. Stand firm. Refuse to do anything which you feel is damaging to your physical or mental health. Pay the price you have to pay for such firmness early in the relationship, before the price gets steeper.

ᘓ *My husband kept saying that if I really loved him, I would do whatever he wanted. It started with me turning over my small inheritance to him. Then he wanted me to give up speaking to friends and family members. He wouldn't let me go to classes or do my art work. If I argued with him, he would explode at me. I was afraid of my own husband! Finally I realized that my passivity was only making things worse. I had to set limits and go back to doing things which gave me joy. I insisted on going to shiurim to gain inspiration. I also insisted that we go for marriage counseling. He yelled and screamed. He tried sweet-talking me and he tried intimidating me, but I wouldn't budge. He now has to choose whether he wants me on my terms or not at all, and I am feeling relieved that I am no longer his victim."*

Some think *shalom bayis* is synonymous with giving in. This is a naive and dangerous attitude. You cannot "make peace" with someone who is trying to kill your spirit. Cancer does not disappear by pretending it does not exist.

❑ DO THINGS THAT BRING YOU JOY: When you live in a poisonous atmosphere you must do everything possible to nurture yourself. Otherwise, you will sink into the victim role, feeling totally helpless, bitter and depressed. Find creative activities which restore your spirit, self-esteem and self-confidence. Be around people who care about you in order to offset the effect of the hostile radiations at home. Find an inspiring charity project to lift you above the pain.

Note: You must keep your activities secret, for abusers will either ridicule anything that brings you joy or thwart your plans.

❑ IF YOU ARE MARRIED TO AN ABUSER, EXPECT YOUR CHILDREN TO BE AFFECTED NO MATTER HOW LOVING YOU ARE: It is the loving parent who is likely to be scorned by the children. If you are quietly submissive, they accuse you of being weak and not protecting them, but if you argue back, they blame you for provoking the explosions or beatings which follow. If you stay, you are considered weak-willed, but if you leave, you are termed a "rebellious wife" or a deserter. They may insult you and even hit you because seeing you being treated with disrespect makes them think this is permissible behavior. They see insults as a sign of being powerful, and power is very important to abused children.

Children of abuse may become either abusers or victims, for they grow up thinking that abusive behavior is normal and even necessary. Yet removing them from this atmosphere may not be easy either.

❑ EVEN IF YOU ARE VERY UNHAPPY, YOU MAY SPEND MANY YEARS IN "DIVORCE LIMBO." Getting divorced is very traumatic. So is not getting divorced. Either way, there is damage. To see a parent crushed by another parent is devastating. Yet most people in this situation stay together because of the need to appear normal and successful. They have realistic fears that divorce will mean:

> ❧ Damaging the children's trust in people.

> ❧ Losing the children to the spouse who has more money.

> ❧ Not having quality or quantity time with the children.

> ❧ Not finding good *shidduchim* (spouses) for the children.

> ❧ Loss of social respectability (female divorcees are often scorned, while male divorcés are

usually considered good catches).

ୡ Social ostracism (female divorcees are often shunned by former friends, who may view them as a threat to their own marriages).

ୡ Loneliness (especially on Shabbos, holidays and at social events).

ୡ Impoverishment (70% of divorced women live in poverty).

ୡ Being left an *agunah* (a woman who cannot obtain a Jewish bill of divorce [*get*] from her spouse).

ୡ Being trapped in ongoing legal battles which drain the victim physically, emotionally and financially.

ୡ Seeing one's small income eaten up by money-hungry lawyers.

ୡ Having one's life in the hands of social workers and judges who are often scornful of the victim. In general, outsiders tend to disbelieve the victims of abuse and to side with the abuser. One reason for this is that by the time most victims seek divorce, they are often "shell-shocked," having been dehumanized and robbed of all sense of self-worth and self-confidence. As the symptom-bearers, they are anxious, depressed and isolated. They may appear unintelligent and disoriented and may be suffering from a stress-related illness. Most have Post-Traumatic Stress Disorder and are easily provoked to outbursts or tears. In contrast, abusers appear unruffled and calm, making them seem more sane and competent.

It is no surprise that many victims constantly wonder if they are courageous or cowardly for staying. It is an agonizing decision. However, there is no question that you must leave if:

    ᘒ Your spouse is molesting the children.

    ᘒ There is ongoing physical violence.

    ᘒ You have no will to live and keep praying to die soon.

❑ KNOW THAT ABUSE CAN CONTINUE AFTER DIVORCE: Even if someone does have the money for a divorce, divorce may not end the abuse, especially if children are involved. Abusers often get custody of the children since they are likely to have more money, hire the best lawyers and are adept at lying. They may bribe the children with expensive gifts or poison the children's minds against the other parent.

Even if the victim does get custody, the abuser may continue to stalk her/him or threaten kidnapping and financial ruin.

❑ EXPECT SECONDARY WOUNDING FROM THOSE WHO BLAME YOU: If your spouse were suffering from cancer, God forbid, you would be given untold support and sympathy. But when a spouse suffers from "cancer of the spirit," a far different response is evoked. Abuse is a reality which most people would prefer to avoid. People generally assume that it is the job of the woman to do anything to keep a marriage intact and that if a marriage fails, it is because of some deficiency on her part.

ೞ *"All the advisors I turned to said, 'Just give in. Be
more respectful. Don't pay attention to what he
says.' That was like telling me not to pay attention to an earthquake. When I became depressed,
people kept telling me to be hopeful, as if facing
reality is a crime. I just don't understand how people think a person can live with abuse and not be
affected by it."*

It is a sad fact of life that the one who complains is often
the one who is blamed. Blaming the victim means not
having to think about the reality of random, unexplainable
and unavoidable evil. If the victim is somehow at fault,
then the abuse somehow makes sense, seems fair, explain-
able and avoidable.

This is why victims are often told, "It's because you're too
emotional, demanding, messy, talkative, quiet, fat, not
submissive enough or too submissive, etc." An abused
wife may try to change herself by losing weight or becoming
more silent and submissive. An abused husband might
take over the household chores and never say a word of
protest, even when his wife throws tantrums. When nothing
works, victims are often told, "You aren't trying hard
enough."

Because it feels good to be optimistic, outsiders think there
must be a solution. They provide all kinds of advice, not
realizing that this advice implies that the victim is to blame.
For example:

> "Swallow the pain and don't complain."

> "You just don't know how to communicate —
> when you find the right key, everything will be
> fine."

"The whole problem is that you expect too much."

"You're taking it too seriously."

"Make yourself into a nothing so he will feel like a something."

"A truly righteous woman can change the most awful man. If you were really righteous, he'd be fine. The fact that he's not, means you're not really righteous, in which case you must deserve to be abused." [*Note:* Though this principle might be true in normal marriages, it does not apply to emotionally disturbed people. There must be some degree of mutuality to make a marriage work.]

"It takes two to fight. Just don't respond. If you stop provoking, everything will be fine." [*Note:* Yes, provocations do exist. It is very difficult to live with someone who is irresponsible, messy, lazy, unstable or wasteful. An emotionally healthy spouse will suffer, but will not become abusive. In contrast, a person with aps can have the most loving, competent spouse and still find excuses to criticize, if not some present failure, then some past mistake. Or, they might complain that the spouse is too successful! There is no way to avoid "provoking" them since one's very existence is a "provocation." The excuses they give — messes, noise, spending habits, weight — are simply rationalizations they use to feel superior and powerful.]

"But s/he is such a lovely person! A pillar of the community. It can't be. You must be exaggerating. You must have imagined it. It can't be true."

"Deaden yourself emotionally. Then you won't get hurt."

"If you're really nice, s/he will be nice back. It's your job to cure him/her."

"Stop dwelling on the past. Just forgive and forget. It's a sin to feel resentful. When someone loves you, anything they do is okay and they should be forgiven no matter what they do."

"Be grateful that you have a spouse."

"If you just knew how to communicate properly, s/he'd be fine. You have to know how to talk to the person."

"You must have sinned. God only punishes bad people."

"You must have an unconscious need to be abused. You wouldn't be abused if you weren't asking for it."

"You can stop it if you want. Just tell him/her that you won't stand for any more abuse."

Some of this advice would be fine if you were dealing with a normal person. But when an abuser is involved, such advice is dangerous. Before giving advice, people should verify whether or not the person they are speaking to is a victim of abuse.

❑ KEEP AN ABUSE JOURNAL: You must keep a journal of abusive events. Note the time and circumstances. In the case of a court battle, this will be essential, as, when questioned, you may be too distraught to remember or not be able to convince others that these incidents really happened.

❑ MAKE A NEW FAMILY FOR YOURSELF: For the sake of your mental health, give up trying to get through to people who are nasty to you. Whether or not someone likes you is in God's hands, not yours. You need to grow and put your energies into worthwhile pursuits. Whether or not your spouse matures is beyond your control. Let go. There are so many lonely singles, divorcees, widows and victims of abuse who are longing for companionship. "Adopt" brothers, sisters, children, parents and grandparents. If you are after divorce, invite these people for meals and holidays. Invest your time in giving love to those who can appreciate it.

❑ Endorse yourself throughout the day: If you live with an abuser, know that:

      03 Every time you smile is a victory. (Do not expect to smile in his/her presence.)

      03 Every act of love you do for yourself is a victory. (Do not expect to feel loving in his/her presence.)

      03 Every healthy thought and act is a victory.

Getting Yourself Under Control

ONE

UNDERSTANDING
WHAT DRIVES YOU

D o you find yourself constantly judging, grading, rating, comparing and condemning? If so, you have an addiction which can be cured. The fact that you feel ashamed and are aware that your behavior is harmful means that you do not have a hardened abusive personality, but rather that you have not yet learned how to deal positively with your own negative impulses. There are few more difficult yet rewarding acts than to go against the natural impulse to respond to hurt by hurting back.

A story which illustrates the great spiritual reward we get from doing so is told in *Sippurei Ha-Ramach,* by Rabbi Mordechai Chaim of Slonim. Rabbi Pinchas of Koritz had a friend who was noted for never causing others pain. When this friend was close to death, Rabbi Pinchas asked him to return to him in a dream after he died and tell him what it was like to pass from this world to the next. Afterwards, this friend did come back to him in a dream and told him that after he was buried, he rose to heaven. There was a question as to whether or not he would have to undergo the usual cleansing process which is normally incumbent on mortals, when suddenly a voice rang out saying, "Because you have been so careful to avoid *ona'as devarim*, you go straight to Gan Eden."

IF YOU ARE A CONDEMNAHOLIC

A "condemnaholic" is a person who feels driven to control or improve people through continual criticism, usually in order to feel superior. Criticizing like this is a compulsive habit, and not one that is easy to control. Research has shown that if the condemnaholic views himself as having a destructive addiction, he can better gain control over it through ongoing acts of self-control and the guidance of a therapist.

If you are aware of being hyper-critical, you have already taken the first step to change! Do not condemn yourself for having an impulse to judge others. This is a natural tendency which every person must learn to control. Simply being aware, in a neutral way, of the habit and not acting on it helps it fade. Then put your thumb up in a victory sign each time you praise someone or restrain your urge to condemn, yell, criticize or indulge in any other form of emotional cruelty.

Try to understand why you condemn. Judging yourself as either superior or inferior is a way of staying isolated — from both man and God. Why would you do this? Ask yourself:

ATTACHMENT DISORDER:
"Do I yearn for closeness but fear rejection?"

If you suffered childhood abuse, you were "burned" so often by people that you are afraid to get close, certain that you would be burned again. You resolve this dilemma by constantly picking on others as a way of connecting to them and, at the same time, keeping them distant. This pattern can be broken only by forcing yourself to mention the positive in others and expressing love, even insincerely at first.

EXCESSIVE DESIRE FOR CONTROL:
"Do I think I must control people in order to stay close to them?"

If so, know that you will only alienate them. They will resist you to maintain their sense of identity.

EXCESSIVE RESPONSIBILITY:
"Do I think it's my task in life to change others?"

If so, know that other people's *middos* are their business, not yours. Yes, you are required to help your children develop good *middos*, but you can't do that by displaying bad *middos*! Your task is to have unconditional love for them — then they will improve to the extent that they are capable of doing so, given their personalities, passions and predispositions.

LACK OF *EMUNAH*:
"Do I think the world is essentially hostile and, therefore, am I always seeing every loss as unnecessary and unfair?"

If so, resolve right now to *bless* every stressful event, no matter how minor or major, as given to you by Hashem out of love, so that you can elevate yourself by displaying good *middos*. He wants you to know your own greatness! Train your mind to respond to stress by repeating to yourself or out loud, "*Thank You for giving me a chance to improve my middos!*" At first, your family members may think you are a bit strange for saying these words, but do not let this concern you. The important thing is that this mind-set keeps you calm by connecting you to the truth: you alone give a positive meaning to your particular frustrations and disappointments by seeing them as opportunities to strengthen yourself spiritually. So, whenever you feel hurt, say that phrase out loud. If a child refuses to help or makes a mess, say it. Then you can solve the problem calmly.

LACK OF SKILLS:

"My kids aren't like other kids. They are abnormally wild, messy, defiant and demanding. Therefore, being nice will not work. They cooperate only if I scream or hit."

Anger is quick, but creates so much resistance that you need far more time to get cooperation than if you would use positive reinforcement techniques like praise, charts and prizes. (See *Raising Children to Care*, by this author, for non-abusive tactics to get kids to cooperate.) Your children need your love. Only then will they be more cooperative, not vice-versa.

LONELINESS:

"Do I try to make people into copies of myself so I won't feel alone?"

This won't work. Compatibility does not require sameness. It requires that you truly appreciate your differences as well as your points of similarity. Focus on what you do have in common. Express verbal and written appreciation for what is positive about others.

EXCUSE MENTALITY:

"Do I think that every upset is a reasonable justification to explode?"

Yes, it is much more difficult to control ourselves when we are nervous, hungry, tired, financially stressed, "hormonally challenged," or under time pressure. But God said, "Don't hurt others..." (*Vayikra* 25:17). So we know that it must be possible.

PARANOIA:
"Do I think that everyone is deliberately out to hurt me?"

To you, every First Degree hurt seems like a Third Degree burn. If a child awakens you, makes a mess or has a tantrum, you jump to "Third Degree — deliberate." If your spouse is tired, makes a request or cannot fulfill your request, you again think "*Davka*, Deliberate, Third Degree." To change this pattern, you must constantly give others the benefit of the doubt, repeating to yourself over and over, "They are doing the best they can with the tools they have at this moment."

Children are messy, noisy, demanding and defiant not to hurt you but because this is how children are. Teach them how to cooperate by demonstrating good *middos* yourself. Be firm but loving. Anger does nothing but generate more defiance.

PERFECTIONISM:
"Do I criticize because I think only perfect people deserve love?"

If so, realize that the Torah does not say, "Love your fellowman as yourself — only if he lives up to your expectations." The Torah simply says, "Love!"

Constantly re-educate your mind by thinking thoughts which make you feel loving and forgiving. (*Living with Difficult People*, by this author, will be of help to you.)

TWO

PUTTING
YOURSELF IN THE
DRIVER'S SEAT

There are any number of things that you can do to help get your thoughts and your impulses under control:

❏ SEE A NEURO-PSYCHIATRIST: If you have wild mood swings and sudden outbursts you may have a hormonal disorder or ADHD (Attention Deficit Hyperactivity Disorder). There are numerous medicines which can help calm you, such as Prozac, Wellbutrin, Ritalin and Lithium. There are also natural products which can help: DLPA (phenylalanine), GLA (Gamma Linoleic Acid), L-glutamine and L-tyrosine and natural lithium, to name a few.

If you have hypoglycemia, you need a special diet to help stabilize your moods.

You may also need therapy to give you the ongoing support you need to overcome your addiction to condemning others, which stems from a fear of closeness. Many people have "attachment disorders" of this kind, usually due to some early disturbance in the mother-child bond. There is nothing shameful about needing help. Be proud of yourself for being responsible and having the courage to recognize the problem and to make an effort to solve it.

❑ AVOID ANGER LIKE AN EX-ALCOHOLIC AVOIDS ALCOHOL: Realize that you have an addiction. And addictions require self-control. Do not expect the process to be easy. Every day brings its share of disappointments, losses, messes, and heartbreaks. Each time this happens, tell yourself, "This is a spiritual test. This is an opportunity to express love and self-control, instead of my old patterns of hostility and fear."

If a small child does something truly dangerous, it is probably appropriate to yell. Otherwise, don't. Condemning people does not get them to change. It only makes them angry and anxious. Simply noticing your bad habit will help it fade.

Pledge a sum of money to *tzedakah* which you promise to give each time you explode.

❑ BREAK YOUR COMPULSION TO RESPOND: You don't have to respond to every little thing that goes wrong. Choose not to go ballistic over trivialities. Choose to focus only on those things which have eternal value, i.e., *mitzvos* and *middos*. Make a firm decision right now to view the following as trivialities which you will either ignore or solve calmly:

WASTED FOOD:

Yes, it is wrong to deliberately waste food, but it is not a terrible sin which calls for an explosion. People often take more than they can eat. Forcing someone to overeat so as not to waste food is not healthy for them. Don't turn it into a big deal.

CLOTHING:

Let children choose what to wear and allow them to have their own taste, as long as it is modest and within your price range.

MEALS:

Let family members choose the food they like, within reason. Forcing children to eat is abusive.

MESSES:

Clean up messes without emotionalism. If you have obsessive-compulsive disorder, get professional help instead of driving everyone crazy with neurotic demands.

MINOR MONEY LOSSES:

Don't explode over minor amounts.

The Hebrew word for trivial is *kikyoni*. Children enjoy using this word. Be proud every time you restrain the urge to kick someone (yourself included) over something which is *kikyoni*!

If you suffer from paranoia, every minor loss will seem to have catastrophic implications. For example, unwashed dishes means, "He doesn't love me." You may need therapy to change your way of thinking.

❑ REPLAY THE SCENE WHEN A CHILD IS DISRESPECTFUL: Disrespect from children must not be tolerated. However, this does not justify screaming and other forms of verbal abuse. Practice in front of the mirror until you develop a noncondemnatory tone which allows you to say firmly, but with love: "I cannot allow you to speak to me disrespectfully. I really want to hear what you have to say. I care about what you like and dislike. But you must speak respectfully even if you are upset. Now, tell me what you want in a respectful tone of voice."

If a child is too upset to cooperate, wait for a calm moment and then allow him to replay the scene. You might have to give a child the words he should be using: "If you don't want to do a chore, don't say, 'Get off my back.' Say, 'Ima,

I have so many things to do right now. Can we make a compromise?' Now, say these words to me."

If a child doesn't like the food you have prepared, say, "When you don't like what I've made, tell me, 'I appreciate that you made me this meal. But I don't like this. Please let me make myself something else.' Or, 'Please can you make me something else.' Now, I'm going to place the disliked food in front of you and I want you to repeat those words in a respectful tone."

❑ AVOID HARSH PUNISHMENTS: Don't punish for trivialities or misjudgments. Punishments should teach, not enrage the child even more. Our Sages tell us not to punish children by depriving them of food. Do not punish a child for lack of religious observance, as this will only make him hate religion.

Some children are cooperative by nature, while others are more defiant by nature. Parents of the latter type of child must find ways to make chores pleasant and should even give small rewards when the children are little. One trick: put on a cassette and ask them to finish a chore before the song finishes. To encourage responsibility as they get older, a parent can keep a written record of a child's most difficult acts of self-discipline. Read the list frequently to him.

❑ SCREAM SOMETHING POSITIVE: If you feel you must scream, try screaming, "This is not the way a *ben/bas Melech* should act!" "We're going to have to find a very good solution to this." "I want you to know that I'm really working very hard to control myself right now."

Screamers should exercise regularly. The stresses of daily life cause the build-up of certain toxic substances in the bloodstream which are released within twenty minutes of vigorous exercise. Exercise also produces endorphins, which will elevate your mood.

❑ ENTHUSIASTICALLY ENDORSE GOOD *MIDDOS*: People want more than anything for others to value them. Love means accepting and cherishing people as they are, not as you want them to be. If you express appreciation for the little things others do for you, they will do those things more often.

Make a realistic plan which involves specific actions. For example:

ଔ Look at your watch; every half hour, say something nice to someone. It can be about yourself, another person or life itself!

ଔ Promise yourself to smile five times a day to a family member when you don't really feel like it.

ଔ Keep a shoe box in the kitchen and have yourself and family members write down positive things they see you or others do each day. Write each item on a separate piece of paper and drop them all into the shoe box. Write at least five notes a week for each person. Read them at the Shabbos table.

If you start early enough, you can strengthen any positive character trait in a child. This requires that you note the negative, but reinforce the positive with enthusiasm. For example, you can encourage:

RESPONSIBILITY:

Write down in a notebook each time the child is on time, helpful or responsible. Praise him enthusiastically and say,

"You came home on time! That was so responsible of you!"
"You got exactly what I asked you to get in the store. That
was so responsible." Write him a note and put it in his
lunch bag.

NEATNESS:
Write down the times he does put things in order.

SHARING:
Write down the smallest act of kindness, sharing or consideration of other people's needs.

SELF-CONTROL:
Ask him each day, "What was your biggest act of self-re-
straint?" Write it down!

COURAGE:
Write down any act of initiative or honesty.

ENTHUSIASM, PATIENCE AND LOVE
LEAD TO REAL CHANGE

New cells are formed in your brain by writing, so take the
time to write down the positive. Writing down the positive
strengthens the memory of the positive in your mind. You
might even mail a letter once in a while to the child to
express your appreciation of an especially difficult act of
self-discipline. This is very impressive to him. You might
think that writing is very time-consuming. In truth, you will
save hours of arguments and agony. Every parent who
keeps such a notebook is surprised at the positive results.

❑ FAKE IT: All change is difficult and feels awkward at
first. It's perfectly fine to pretend to be loving, to wear
a fake smile and put on a pleasant voice even when
you are upset.

❑ PRACTICE HAVING LOVE IN YOUR HEART: You are used to feeling angry, hurt and resentful, as these emotions seem safe and familiar from childhood. Now make a conscious choice to give love. Start with non-threatening things, like birds, trees and flowers. Allow yourself to enjoy them. Allow yourself to feel deep love and appreciation for Hashem, who made these creations. Notice how you can create the feeling of love on your own, at any time, simply by feeling gratitude.

Next, feel appreciation for the family members who are not threatening to you at the moment. Forgive others for not being all you want them to be. Finally, and what may be hardest, feel love for yourself, as you are. Forgive yourself for not being all you hoped to be. Let your heart fill with love — abundant love. Whenever possible, tell your family members:

> "You need my help? Good. Thank you for giving me the opportunity to do a chesed."

> "I made this meal for you because I love you."

> "I'm driving you to your lesson because I really love you."

> "I'm controlling myself and not hitting because I love you."

Note: Family members may not trust you at first. Be patient. Allow them to express the pain which has built up over the years. Listen. Validate non-judgmentally. Stay loving.

❑ ASK HASHEM TO HELP YOU OVERCOME THIS DESTRUCTIVE HABIT: Like all addictions, you cannot win this battle without help. Ask for:

ଔ Strength to control yourself.

ଔ A fighting spirit to persist in this struggle.

ଔ An end to your sense of isolation and bitterness.

ଔ An ever-expanding ability to express love.

ଔ A sense of God's presence.

(*Thirty Seconds to Emotional Health,*[*] by this author, will help you become a more loving person.)

> Whenever you feel the urge
> to indulge in *ona'as devarim*
> — whether to control something
> or someone who cannot be controlled,
> or to feel superior —
> get yourself back in control
> by repeating,
> "Hashem, please restore me to sanity,"
> until you calm down.

---

* Feldheim Publishers, 1996.

Helping Children Deal
with Verbal Abuse

There are many emotionally disturbed, nasty-tempered, hostile people in the world who have a negative effect on the lives of children. Their behavior is especially damaging when they are in a position of trust, such as a parent, teacher or older sibling, who is supposed to be a source of love, guidance or protection. The psychological damage is more severe when the victim is told he must respect or love the person who is hurting him! This is terribly confusing to a child.

Some children respond to the tension by engaging in hostile acts such as stealing, lying, running away, damaging property and behaving with hostility toward other children and animals. Others become self-hating, depressed and suicidal. Some become obsessively neat. Still others try to act like saintly models of religiosity, adopting a seriousness inappropriate for their age group and disavowing all forms of pleasure. This is an attempt to assuage feelings of being total failures or evil monsters, a self-image internalized from the abuser.

In order to feel safe, children tend to assume that whatever adults do is permissible. The horror which we should feel when another human being is devalued is erased when children grow up thinking it is normal to explode angrily or refuse to speak for days when one is upset, to punish harshly for some minor infraction, to mock and belittle others and to pick at every fault one sees in others. Physical attacks also come to be seen as unavoidable, necessary and acceptable when they occur on a frequent basis.

Yet the one who complains is likely to be the one who is blamed. Children are often told that they provoked the attack, which makes it seem legitimate. Justifying abuse teaches children to tolerate it and engage in it themselves.

Children must know that even if other people have bad *middos*, they have to have good *middos*. However, they cannot deal with the pain in a healthy manner without guidance and healthy role models.

When a child is subject to abuse, he needs your support, validation and protection, not whitewashing or minimizing. Many parents are too tolerant of verbal abuse, shrugging it off nonchalantly as insignificant, invalidating the child's right to be in pain and telling him, "It's nothing. Forgive and forget." While it is often impossible to educate the offender, forthright action is necessary to prevent further abuse. This may involve excluding certain people from your home or changing schools.

The following suggestions will help:

STRENGTHENING A CHILD'S SELF-WORTH

❑ OFTEN USE WORDS LIKE LOVE, CONFIDENCE AND FAITH:

> "Have the confidence that Hashem will give you the strength to get through this difficulty."

> "Hashem loves you just as you are. And so do I!"

When a child makes a good decision, even about something very minor, such as what to eat or wear, point out his ability to choose wisely. Say,

> "That was a good decision. Doesn't it feel good to know that you can trust yourself to make good decisions?"

> "I trust that you have the inner wisdom to make the right decision," when he asks you to decide

for him (what to wear, what color to draw with, whether to go to a friend's house, etc.).

"Relax. There's no right or wrong with that decision, so don't worry. Whatever you decide is fine."

"Plan, act, and don't look back! Don't obsess about the decision once it's made; just focus on the fact that you had the courage to make the decision."

"I see that you're a responsible child. I know that because you _____. It feels good to know that I can rely on you."

"Hashem determines your value, not people's opinions."

"Let me show you our family newspaper. In this newspaper, I write down all the special blessings of the week and your acts of courage, self-control and consideration. You belong to this family and we all work together to make the environment safe for everyone."

"You're good at _____."

"It makes me proud to see you exercising self-control."

"I can't take away all your pain, but I can be here to share it with you. I care about what you feel."

"That took a lot of courage! You're a courageous kid."

"Look how industrious you are! You have a great deal of tenacity and devotion. You'll do a lot for the world."

"You have a lot of self-discipline. I noticed that you controlled yourself instead of _____."

"Thank you for being so considerate. You have a good heart."

"Yes, it's painful, but I have complete confidence that you can function with pain. That's what courage is all about."

"Relax. There's no danger. I agree that it is distressing, but it's not dangerous."

"Mistakes are not catastrophes. They're learning experiences. We all make mistakes."

"Thank you for cooperating. I like the fact that I can trust you to be there for me."

"Let's call the Rav and let him decide. We can trust him."

"I know this is painful, but let's focus on solutions."

Buy a simple crown. Put it on his head. Tell him, "You are now Shelomo *Ha-melech*, the wisest man in the world." Then tell him the problem he is upset about and say, "Oh, wise King, please give me a solution now to this problem we have."

For severe grouches: "I'll give you a star every time you say something positive about someone. When you collect a certain number of them, we'll buy you something you need."

If he has trouble separating fact from fantasy, say, "If I told you that the moon was purple, would that be a lie or the truth?" Frequently ask him such questions.

❑ PROTECT: Say, "What she said to you was not okay. No wonder you feel hurt." If possible, say, "Come with me while I tell him that he is not allowed to talk to you like that." If someone pinches your child's cheek (hard), say, "That hurts. Don't do that to my child." This teaches children to be assertive in protecting themselves from hurtful behavior.

Keep the child away from repeat offenders, including older siblings who belittle or are physically abusive. Children can be extremely vicious to each other, especially those who are unpopular or handicapped in any way. Don't tell your children to "work it out on your own" if they are being abused. Children can become suicidally depressed and retain life-long feelings of inferiority from being bullied. Call in appropriate authorities, including the police, a lawyer or a therapist, if necessary.

❑ SHOW THEM HOW TO IDENTIFY REFINED VS. UNREFINED PEOPLE: On the one hand, you do not want your children to think that every offense is an act of abuse. You don't want them to judge others too quickly. They should be reminded often that if the person was not *intentionally* cruel, then no sin was committed, even if they were hurt by what occurred. On the other hand, you want them to protect themselves, to know that just as the sea is full of nasty sharks and gentle dolphins, so too is the world full of both of those types of people. Children can make a list of the differences between the two. For example:

SHARK RULES:

Hurt whenever you can. Never apologize. Blame others for everything. Argue about everything. Boast. Mock and belittle others. Turn every mistake into a catastrophe so people feel like criminals.

DOLPHIN RULES:

Help whenever you can. Apologize, even if you didn't do it on purpose. Stroke those in pain. Make peace. Turn mistakes into learning experiences. Forgive. Love. Have fun. Enjoy life.

❑ VALIDATE THEIR PAIN: An insult is a mini-death experience. Don't say, "It's nothing." This will only teach the child to invalidate his own and others' emotional pain. Don't automatically say, "S/he didn't mean it," unless you know for sure that this is true.

If the person is usually kind-hearted, do ask the child, "Are you sure she meant to hurt you?" Or say, "I'm so sorry. It hurts. I sympathize with you. This has often happened to me." If you can't do anything, say, "I can't change the situation, but I can share your pain. We'll work together to make the people more aware of how terrible *ona'as devarim* is."

❑ GIVE CHILDREN, ESPECIALLY SENSITIVE ONES, COPING TACTICS:

Tell him that the one who does not return an insult with an insult has all his sins wiped away and is especially beloved by God (*Rosh Hashanah* 17a). Be really enthusiastic about his refusal to engage in *ona'as devarim*.

Provide books, such as *Love Your Neighbor*, by Rabbi Zelig

Pliskin, which tell inspiring stories about how our Sages responded to insults with dignity. Help them understand how a person can choose not to be thrown off-center by insults by attaching himself to a higher truth.

Have the child pray for the one with emotional problems.

Enroll a picked-on child in a self-defense class; this will reduce his anxiety and build his self-confidence.

Teach children when and when not to judge. They should know that critical judgments are necessary in issues of morality, health and Halachah. Provide examples of when it is important to judge (e.g., how to identify people who are dangerous and untrustworthy). Teach them to ask themselves the question, "Do I really need to protect myself from this person? Or am I engaging in ona'as devarim, putting others down for no reason?"

❑ DO NOT EXCUSE ABUSE: Don't be so quick to say, "He's having a bad day and that's why he's out of control." This makes children think that if you can come up with a good enough excuse, then it's okay to offend people. Of course, if a usually kind person is struggling with a gloomy mood, say, "She is having a bad day. Let's be extra nice to her."

❑ MAKE YOUR HOME ENVIRONMENT SAFE: Just as being poor is no excuse to steal, being tired, hungry or nervous is no excuse to hurt people's feelings. Let your family members know that just as you do not allow non-kosher food in your home, you do not allow non-kosher talk to enter.

If you slip and hurt someone's feelings, quickly apologize. Say, "It is wrong to hurt people's feelings. Let's replay the scene. This time, I'll respond in a more civilized way." It is very important for children to see that you, too, put forth the effort to control your own harmful impulses.

If a child hurts your feelings, say, "That kind of talk is not allowed. Let's replay the scene. Tell me what is bothering you, but say it respectfully." (See *Raising Children to Care* by this author for numerous tactics to help children get along with each other.) Replay the scene as soon as possible. If the child is too upset to respond, write yourself a note and then replay the scene with the child after he has calmed down.

❑ ENCOURAGE CHILDREN TO SAY POSITIVE THINGS ABOUT THEMSELVES AND EACH OTHER, ESPECIALLY NOTING THEIR ACTS OF KINDNESS AND SELF-CONTROL: When one sibling does something for another, have the recipient write a little note of thanks. Write the note yourself if the child is too young to write and have him draw a picture instead of signing his name. Children should also writes notes of thanks to parents and teachers as well.

❑ PROTECT CHILDREN FROM ABUSIVE TEACHERS AND PRINCI- PALS: Some children have a tendency to exaggerate what they experience and enjoy saying *lashon hara* about their teachers. This must never be allowed. On the other hand, some teachers undermine the self-esteem of their students, either deliberately or through carelessness.

The task of transmitting information is secondary to their essential role in teaching ethical behavior and enhancing children's self-esteem, for most future emotional problems are rooted in poor self-esteem.

Teachers who are critical, hot-tempered or mean should not be in the classroom. They can be especially cruel to the learning-disabled and resort to shaming tactics, punishments and violence in the mistaken belief that this will get children to learn. Some are downright sadistic and enjoy picking on those who are weaker and helpless. Do not believe those who tell you that our Sages encourage beatings! Our Sages admonish parents and teachers to be gentle and kind and to punish lightly, "with only a shoelace" (*Bava Basra* 21b). It is abhorrent to use Torah to justify abuse.

Abusive teachers and principals will give a million excuses to justify abuse, including telling you, "You're pampering your children," or, "It's good for them. It prepares them for the real world." It is your job as a parent to stand by your child and make sure that he or she is not subjected to verbal abuse, or any other type of abuse, in school. Do not ignore your child's reports of verbal abuse. Take action:

a. VERIFY THE FACTS:
Call the teacher to clarify if what you child thinks was said was actually said. Judge favorably before you make the call. Children, like all of us, may exaggerate or mis-hear because of their need for excitement and attention. Thus, before making this call you might want to check with another child in the class to hear a different view of the incident.

b. IF THE TEACHER CONFIRMS THAT THE REMARKS WERE ACTUALLY MADE, ASK HIM WHAT HE MEANT BY THEM.
It could be that your child misinterpreted the teacher's comments. If your clarification reveals that the teacher is not careful about refraining from ona'as devarim, you must take concrete steps.

c. BEFORE PROCEEDING, FIND OUT FROM PARENTS OF OTHER CHILDREN IN THE CLASS IF THEY HAVE

ALSO HEARD ABOUT VERBAL ABUSE IN THIS CLASS. Your efforts to change the situation will be more effective if you know that you are not alone. Asking other parents can show you that they feel the same way you do. Sadly, many parents accept *ona'as devarim* as normal, unavoidable or trivial and they do not bother to look into it.

There is no one single method of stopping *ona'as devarim* in the classroom that works for all situations. Some parents have successfully protected their children by: protesting to the teacher that his or her behavior is unacceptable; talking confidentially to the principal; consulting an influential rabbi; complaining to the parents' association; notifying the school board, etc. Despite the apathy, whitewashing and denial which may greet you, be persistent.

> **d.** DEVELOP AN *ONA'AS DEVARIM* UNIT FOR YOUR CHILD'S SCHOOL TO RAISE THE CONSCIOUSNESS OF CHILDREN AND TEACHERS.

> **e.** HAVE YOUR CHILD TESTED FOR ADD-ADHD.

Such children can be so trying that they can drive the most well-meaning teacher to explode unless the teacher is specially trained to deal with such children. Read books to help you and your child's teachers understand this condition. (See *Driven to Distraction and Answers to Distraction*, by Hallowell and Ratey, Pantheon Books, and *You Mean I'm Not Lazy, Stupid or Crazy*, by Kelly and Ramundo, Simon & Shuster.) There are numerous organizations that are dedicated to helping both children and adults with ADD.

A free catalogue of supplies can be received by calling: 1-800-962-1141.

No matter what steps you take, verbal abuse in the classroom must be stopped. Do not allow your child's spirit to be destroyed. There are cases where children have required psychiatric help after suffering repeated mocking and shaming at school. If necessary, change classes or find a more sympathetic school.

Post-Traumatic Stress Disorder: It's Not "Just Words"

ONE

RECOGNIZING PTSD

In a healthy relationship, where the total view is positive, the mature person will shrug off an accidental, thoughtless remark made in haste and will forgive the offender. Unfortunately, the average person thinks he should be able to do the same when dealing with real abuse. When he can't, he may blame himself, thinking, "I must be immature or crazy to feel so hurt and enraged. Why can't I just take it?"

Even if you tell yourself, "I won't take it to heart," the heart is instantly affected. The body is very sensitive to any threat. Insults are experienced as attacks, causing adrenaline to flood the entire system. Within minutes of being in the presence of a hostile person, the immune system is weakened, even if the person is not actively hostile at the moment. Thus, in addition to psychological damage, the tension leads to numerous stress-related illnesses. It's like being near a faulty Chernobyl reactor — radiation damage is inevitable.

Furthermore, the abuser keeps telling the victim, "You are crazy — your behavior is so bizarre." A person who is isolated in the home and has no normal points of reference will begin to believe that this is true, especially since any response to abuse is likely to seem strange, if not abnormal to outsiders. Furthermore, since most outsiders condemn the one who is being picked on, the need to keep up a happy front for the world in order not to be seen as a failure, is another major source of stress.

Good communication is what makes people feel safe with each other. But trying to reason with a person suffering from aps is useless, since their responses are not rational. It is not the trauma itself which causes Post-Traumatic Stress Disorder (PTSD) but the sense of helplessness which causes the most psychological damage. When people can take positive action against abuse, they suffer fewer physical and emotional symptoms. When they feel trapped and helpless, PTSD develops.

The major symptoms of PTSD are:

ca Recurrent flashbacks and loss of time-orientation.

ca Sleep disturbances (insomnia, night terrors, frequent awakening in the middle of the night, lethargy, late awakening).

ca An exaggerated "startle response," causing one to overreact with terror or rage which seems out of proportion to the stimulus.

ca A high level of anxiety, with a constant sense of impending physical or emotional collapse or external disaster.

ca Decrease in ability to concentrate, function and respond.

ca Extreme sensitivity to noise.

ca Chronic unhappiness, hopelessness and depression, often to the point of suicidal despair.

ᐧ Stomach disturbances (the constant flow of adrenaline can wear away the stomach lining).

ᐧ Disorganization in action; confusion in thought.

ᐧ Emotional numbness and sense of disconnectedness to loved ones, such as children or others who can give and receive love.

ᐧ A sense of worthlessness, helplessness and paralysis.

ᐧ Strong feelings of shame, guilt and self-hatred.

ᐧ Self-injury alternating with the intense desire to commit violent acts against others.

ᐧ Trembling, nausea and terror upon simply seeing the abuser, even if the latter is not actively abusive at the moment.

ᐧ A sense of being totally alone, abnormal and estranged from the world. [*Note*: since it is the victim who seeks help and is often put on medication, s/he is the one who feels defective, not the abuser.]

In extreme cases: hallucinations, obsessions, compulsions, addictions, hysteria, dissociation and other severe disorders.

Victims of abuse eventually feel repulsion toward the abuser and cannot bear to be in the person's presence. Repulsion is a sign that the victim has reached a certain psychological point of no return. Attempts to patch up a relationship at this point rarely succeed. The damage is simply too profound.

The presence of PTSD means that core damage has occurred, which may not be reversible, and which gets worse the longer the person remains in the presence of the abuser.

If you have signs of PTSD, it is important to reassure yourself that these are signs of abuse and not to think, "I'm really crazy and I therefore deserve abuse." You cannot live close to a leaky nuclear reactor and not be affected. At least now you will know that you are not the crazy one, even if you must take medication to stay calm around the person.

PTSD is most severe when you feel trapped in a no-win situation, when anything you do to please the other person or protect yourself — such as staying or leaving, going to the police or not doing so, seeing a therapist or not doing so, taking medication or not doing so — is all likely to be condemned and make you look bad, wrong, stupid or crazy. This is why you must take action to give yourself a sense of power and value.

RESPECT YOUR LIMITATIONS
WITH HUMILITY AND COURAGE

If you suffer from PTSD, you will sometimes overreact to minor stresses. For example, being in a crowd, even at a happy social event, may evoke intense discomfort. A minor medical procedure may be far more painful for you than for the average patient. A change in your normal routine may arouse intense anxiety. A curt clerk or accidental bump from a stranger may set off the alarms. You may feel emotionally paralyzed or find yourself sweating and trembling around authority figures. When you tell someone that you cannot deal with a certain relative, you may be told,

"What's wrong with you? I get along just fine with him/her."

You are not crazy. You have PTSD, which means that your brain is programmed to respond to stress by flooding your cells with adrenaline. You may not be able to prevent this initial response, but you can prevent it from spiraling into a panic by learning biofeedback techniques to calm yourself as soon as you become aware of your nervous symptoms.

Why you have PTSD and others do not is because God gave you an extremely sensitive nervous system. Do not be ashamed of this "handicap." Do not compare yourself to those who can stay calm and cool. Their "internal wiring" is different. Have the humility to admit that you cannot be around certain people without having your nervous symptoms triggered. Yet develop the courage to take on people and projects which enhance your self-confidence and self-respect.

TWO

THOSE LIKELY
TO BE ABUSED

Ｐeople are abused for many reasons. The main positive reason that a person like you may be prone to being abused is that you are a highly spiritual, modest, trusting and self-effacing person, a care-giver who enjoys giving. You are so good-hearted that you assume everyone else is too, underneath it all. Similarly, abusers think everyone is just as cruel as they are, which makes them think they have the right to hurt others. When someone is nice to them, they think the person is manipulative and evil underneath the mask of niceness just as you are certain the abuser is essentially good underneath the mask of nastiness.

Some less positive reasons may be that you:

a. CRAVE CONTACT AT ALL COSTS.
If you were abused as a child, you learned to call abuse "love" because you needed to feel loved. Any attention was better than no attention, even if attention was in the form of insults. Now, you keep trying to get love from people who cannot give it, which is what you did as a child. You keep trying obsessively to get through and make the person understand your feelings and your need for love.

b. ARE A SELF-BLAMER.
You feel like a failure if you can't make everyone happy. If someone dislikes you, you think, "There must be something wrong with me." When someone hurts you, you justify

their behavior, thinking, "I deserved it because, after all, I'm moody, disorganized and needy." If someone blows up angrily, you immediately think, "It's my fault that I got him/her upset." You view yourself as inadequate when you cannot change or heal the other person.

c. HAVE LOW SELF-ESTEEM.

If you are shy and unassertive or emotionally unstable, you may feel you have no choice but to suffer in silence. You may also feel that swallowing your pain in silence is the best solution and is the heroic response. You may feel helpless and view cold, unemotional people as strong and superior and think you need them to protect you from the outside world. Such "protectors" are likely to encourage your feelings of helplessness and ineptness with their constant criticism.

d. ARE QUICK TO EXCUSE.

You tell yourself, "He only insults me a few times a day," "He only gets violent when the bills come in," "I really do feel sorry for him." Being so quick to forgive makes hostile people think that their behavior is okay.

e. INVALIDATE YOUR OWN REALITY.

You feel hurt, but you keep telling yourself, "I shouldn't be upset. I should be able to take it. It's not so bad. Things are improving." You feel guilty when outsiders, who cannot imagine the stress of living with a hostile person, condemn you for not being able to stop the abuse or turn the abuser into a normal human being.

f. ARE A PEOPLE-PLEASER, BENDING OVER BACK-WARDS TO PLEASE.

You always put others first, even when it hurts you. You make super-human efforts to win approval, wondering, "How can I mold myself to be what others want me to be so that they will love me?" You feel guilty whenever you say "No." You are afraid to offend the people who offend you. You think you should and must be able to heal everyone and can get everyone to like you if you just try hard enough.

g. KEEP TRYING OBSESSIVELY TO GET THROUGH.

No matter how many years you have tried and failed, you think, "If I just pray harder, am more submissive, change myself, find the right therapist and the right medication, s/he will change." You think there is a magic key which will get him/her to love you. This is a childish fantasy which cannot be fulfilled.

h. FEAR ABANDONMENT.

You give up your independence, identity and all sources of fulfillment and joy because you are sure that no one else would love you and you fear being alone.

i. SUFFER FROM EXCESSIVE GUILT.

You feel guilty even when you haven't done anything wrong. The fact that you cannot fulfill other people's dreams and demands makes you feel like you are stupid, incompetent and unworthy of respect.

j. ARE "OTHER-REFERENCING," NOT SELF-REFERENCING.

You define yourself in terms of what others think of you, not in terms of any stable, secure sense of your own internal worth.

k. ARE OVERLY OPTIMISTIC.

No matter how nasty a person is to you, you clutch at straws, believing, "S/he does really loves me underneath it all. S/he will change."

Of course, if you constantly indulge in *ona'as devarim* or

other provocative behavior, others may simply not be able to take your behavior. Examples include talking after someone has begged you to stop, constantly nagging them for things they cannot or do not want to change or being unusually irresponsible.

YOU ARE NOT ALONE

David *Ha-melech* was also deeply wounded by malicious words:

"MY SOUL IS AMONG LIONS. AND I LIE DOWN AMONG
THOSE WHO ARE AFLAME, THE SONS OF MEN
WHOSE TEETH ARE SPEARS AND ARROWS
AND THEIR TONGUE A SHARP SWORD"
• TEHILLIM 57:5 •

"HIDE ME FROM THE COUNSEL OF THE WICKED...
WHO HAVE SHARPENED THEIR TONGUE LIKE THE SWORD,
AND AIMED THEIR ARROW, A BITTER WORD,
TO SHOOT IN SECRET AT THE INNOCENT;
SUDDENLY THEY SHOOT HIM AND THEY ARE UNAFRAID"
• TEHILLIM 64:3-5 •

"[THE WICKED] SPEAK FREELY, THEY UTTER MALICIOUS
FALSEHOOD, THEY GLORIFY THEMSELVES..."
• TEHILLIM 94:4 •

"FREE ME, HASHEM FROM THE WICKED...
WHO DEVISE EVIL SCHEMES IN THEIR HEART,
WHO ASSEMBLE DAILY FOR WARS.
THEY HAVE SHARPENED THEIR TONGUE LIKE A SERPENT,
A SPIDER'S VENOM IS UNDER THEIR LIPS...
LET THE MISCHIEF OF THEIR OWN LIPS BURY THEM"
• TEHILLIM 140:2-4,10 •

The only way we can face this pain is to trust that everything we experience comes directly from Him, is for our ultimate good and will somehow ennoble and sensitize us if we maintain our dignity and faith.

The importance of dealing properly with insults is so great that we remind ourselves of the proper attitude three times a day. At the end of the *Amidah* prayer, we say, "Let my soul be silent to those who curse me; let my soul be as dust to all. Open my heart to Your Torah and let my soul eagerly pursue Your commandments." Ultimately, it is our strong trust in God which will enable us to tolerate the pain of feeling dishonored by our fellow men.

Appendices

Spiritual Nourishment: Healing *Neshamah* Phrases

Imagine what you would like a loving friend to tell you and become your own loving friend. Tell yourself:

"I love you just the way Hashem made you, no matter what your imperfections may be."

"I believe in your strengths."

"I love you more than you can possibly imagine."

"Your essence is love and joy. You don't have to change who you are — you just need to discover and express who you are!"

"You have an infinite Godly value. Those who don't value you are blind to the truth."

"You have what you need to be happy right now. In this precious moment, you can find a reason to feel joy and love."

"You are so precious to me."

"I have an unlimited supply of love for you."

"I'm so lucky to have you."

"You're the most important person in my life."

"I'll listen to you at any time."

"You don't have to earn my love. You don't have to prove yourself. My love for you exists at all times."

"I can't take away all the pain in your life, but I can share it with you."

"I notice your acts of self-discipline. I'm so proud of you for your courage, your loving heart, your positive thoughts and actions."

"Every step forward is a victory."

"I accept all your feelings. Express them all to me. I understand how much you are suffering. I am here. I will remind you of your strengths."

"You are important for yourself, not for what you do or give."

"You have your own unique, precious gift to offer the world."

"You belong. You are loved. You deserve to be happy, loved and valued. If others don't provide it, I will."

"You can still give and receive love even when you're feeling confused, overwhelmed or down."

"You're not crazy; you're just afraid of being hurt."

"Let go of your expectations of achieving, complete understanding or total inner peace."

"I will always be here for you. Always. You can always lean on me. I will always support you. I will never fail you."

Add any words you would have wanted to hear from your parents or words you would like to hear from a loving spouse or friend:

_____

_____

_____

_____

_____

Each time you read this page, it will become more deeply ingrained in your consciousness and will eventually become a reality.

DOSAGE:

Think of these phrases as a kind of homeopathic medicine. Take each and every day. Take more if you feel sad or angry. Take as much as you want. It is helpful to keep this page in your *siddur* and read it each day so that your sense of God's love will become real.

APPENDIX B:

Learning To Be More Positive

"A PERSON IS HELPED IN THE WAY HE WANTS TO GO"
• MAKKOS 10B •

Attaining spiritual growth and a connection with God require effort. The effort involved in writing things down demonstrates one's sincerity and commitment to change, and leads to the development of one's positive self-image.

In a loose-leaf notebook, make two columns:

Acts of Self-Control   *Things that Brought Me Joy*

—————————————————   —————————————————
—————————————————   —————————————————
—————————————————   —————————————————
—————————————————   —————————————————
—————————————————   —————————————————
—————————————————   —————————————————
—————————————————   —————————————————

Write down two or three entries a day. Your acts of self-discipline should be things which were always very difficult for you to do. For example, write down every time when you:

        ের Perform a difficult act of kindness for someone.

        ের Overcome the urge to condemn yourself or others.

- ∞ Let go of the urge to dominate or manipulate people.

- ∞ Overcome the urge to compare yourself with others.

- ∞ Forgive and give someone the benefit of the doubt.

- ∞ Display patience under difficult circumstances.

- ∞ Give generously instead of withholding (affection or approval).

- ∞ Take responsibility for some aspect of your life.

- ∞ Set reasonable limits and stand firm.

- ∞ Avoid the urge to lose it and scream, hit, name-call.

- ∞ Realize that a triviality is really a triviality and only a triviality.

- ∞ Accept God's will.

Writing engraves in your brain an awareness of your Godly nature, which is what prompts you to make healthy choices.

In the second column, write down anything in your life for which you are grateful or any little "coincidence" or miracle which occurs. This impresses you with the awareness that there is a God Who is running the universe and that He cares for you enough to provide these little reminders of

His existence and love.

Rabbi Yechezkel Levenstein, *zt"l*, the *mashgiach* of Mir Yeshiva before World War II, would give his children a coin for every incident of *hashgachah pratis* they noticed, in order to strengthen their sense of God's presence. We see from his example how important it is to notice and get enthusiastic about the Godliness in ourselves and in the world.

Mom's Victories

Everyone has an urge to act cruelly and destructively at some time. The more you have been rejected and demeaned by others, the more likely you are to feel like a failure and to feel compelled to shame and devalue others or yourself. Emotional health requires that you feel good about yourself, feel that you have value, no matter what others say to you. To do this, acknowledge your every effort to be kind and self-disciplined. After a few months of writing down these acts of kindness and self-discipline, you will become aware of your Godly essence. Everyone can be a spiritual star. There is a lot of room at the top for those who respond with love, acceptance, compassion and forgiveness.

Below is an example of some entries you might find in a mother's List of Victories.

**OVERCAME ANGER AND THE
DESIRE FOR EXCESSIVE CONTROL:**

❑ Wanted to scream but controlled myself. Then I told the kids out loud that I was controlling myself even though it was difficult.

❑ Didn't force my daughter to choose the eyeglass frames I wanted.

❑ Screamed, but only for two minutes, not for ten minutes.

❑ Went into another room when I felt hostile instead of

venting angrily.

- ❑ Hugged two-year-old really tight when he had a tantrum instead of slapping him.

- ❑ Instead of nagging daughter, didn't say a word even though I felt she was eating too much.

- ❑ Didn't force seven-year-old to finish his meal. Threw away the uneaten portion without making him feel guilty.

- ❑ Let 12-year-old choose the dress she wanted, instead of forcing my will on her. I even told her, "Good decision."

- ❑ Let four-year-old wear her Shabbos shoes to school instead of getting into a power struggle.

- ❑ Begged Hashem to give me a reason to give my husband the benefit of the doubt when he was late.

- ❑ Screamed briefly, but didn't call names when kids were fighting.

- ❑ Said, "It's a triviality," when daughter lost contact lens.

SET FIRM LIMITS WITH RESPECT:

- ❑ Did not give in to four-year-old's tantrum; insisted that he tell me what he wanted in a respectful voice.

- ❑ Told relative that I had to get off the phone instead of continuing to talk when I didn't really want to.

- ❑ Stood firm and made two kids replay the scene after

they spoke disrespectfully to each other.

❑ Politely refused a request from a neighbor which I could not handle instead of taking it on to please her.

❑ Gave up project because family was suffering too much by my absence, even though it would have been exciting.

❑ Insisted that my husband and I have together time on *Rosh Chodesh* instead of complaining about him ignoring me.

❑ Asked husband firmly not to talk on phone during dinner instead of making angry faces at him.

❑ Told my doctor that I wanted a second opinion even though I was afraid to hurt his feelings.

❑ Did not buy expensive schoolbag for daughter, despite her nagging.

OVERCAME LETHARGY AND APATHY:

❑ Had courage to speak with principal about starting an *ona'as devarim* unit in the school.

❑ Did six loads of laundry after the holiday without grumbling.

❑ Was tired, but went for brisk evening walk.

❑ Instead of staying in bed, got up 15 minutes earlier so the morning would go smoothly.

❑ Instead of going back to bed, cleaned the house after

kids left for school.

❑ Went to PTA meeting though I knew I'd hear complaints.

❑ Volunteered to be on neighbor *chesed* committee.

❑ Went to a *shiur* even though I was very down.

❑ Got youngest son tested for learning disabilities — finally!

❑ Took all the kids to the dentist for their check-ups — finally!

❑ Cleaned out closets! Gave old clothes to charity — finally!

❑ Finally went for the blood test I'd been putting off.

OVERCAME ADDICTIVE URGE:

❑ *Daven*ed first, before eating or talking on the phone.

❑ Did not buy on impulse. Came back home to think it over.

❑ Wanted to eat ten cookies, but stopped at two.

❑ Berated myself for only two minutes instead of two hours when I brought the wrong size pants for my son.

❑ Did not condemn myself for being in a bad mood. I accepted God's will that I cannot always feel cheerful.

DISPLAYED LOVE:

❑ Gave a dime to each child each time they said something nice about one another. This was the "trick of the week" for family unity!

❑ Made cake and kugel for sick neighbor.

❑ Apologized to husband after I spoke in anger.

❑ Didn't say a word when I saw my son's messy room, in order to first build a positive relationship with him.

❑ Told my daughter that I understood her pain instead of getting angry when she was in a bad mood.

❑ Played chess with my son toward whom I've felt hostile.

❑ Made a fancy cake to celebrate one week with no screaming.

❑ Put up a page on the fridge to write down the children's positive behavior.

❑ Wrote son a thank-you letter when he cleaned up his room.

❑ Patiently helped nine-year-old with his homework.

❑ Said, "It's a triviality" when son broke his glasses.

❑ Said eleven positive things to my family members today!

❑ Accepted God's will that I have a learning-disabled child instead of pitying myself and condemning the child.

- ❑ Smiled a lot though I've been up for three nights with sick child.

- ❑ Agreed to invite husband's relatives for the holidays.

- ❑ Peeled apple for teenager just to show I love her.

- ❑ Accepted God's will when I didn't get the job I wanted. Kept telling myself that "it's for the best. God loves me."

- ❑ Wrote in my notebook!

- ❑ Said *Tehillim* in the doctor's office instead of getting angry about him being late.

- ❑ Gave grouchy neighbor the benefit of the doubt.

- ❑ Did not say *lashon hara* about a relative to my sister.

- ❑ Went to visit relative in hospital.

- ❑ Started using EMETT language out loud.

- ❑ Said, "I respect your feelings" to child who was upset.

- ❑ When son had a tantrum, kept repeating, "Thank you for giving me the opportunity to work on my *middos.*" The words calmed me and my son!

These are all major spiritual victories!

Mom's Gratefulness List: Hashem Loves Me!

People who have been repeatedly hurt tend to see the universe as hostile and, therefore, to focus on what is wrong and to expect more pain. To change this attitude, ask yourself each day, "What brought me joy today? What special blessing am I grateful for? What little miracles occurred, such as narrowly missing being in an accident or benefitting from some event which seems, on the surface, to be merely a coincidence?"

Writing reinforces the new awareness that "Perhaps God does love me after all, despite all He has put me through." Writing makes the presence of a benevolent God a reality. After a few months of expressing gratitude with two or three written entries, there will be a shift in your consciousness toward greater trust in God's love for you.

Below is an example of some entries you might find in a mother's Gratefulness List.

❑ Having Torah!

❑ There was no one to take my heavy bags of groceries into the house. After I said some *Tehillim*, a boy suddenly appeared and helped me!

❑ Daughter said I deserve a prize for being so calm! Hooray!

❑ Got flowers from husband for Shabbos.

❑ Got lost and someone took me all the way to the

place I needed.

❑ Had a good night's sleep!

❑ Seeing the kids playing nicely together for a few minutes!

❑ Seeing my son *daven*ing.

❑ My daughter said, "Can I help you, Mom?"

❑ Son used his allowance to buy me a gift.

❑ Having a very caring neighbor right next door.

❑ MIRACLE: No line in the post office!

❑ Told the kids to clean the kitchen before the song ended and they did!

❑ Son was sympathetic when I was in pain.

❑ Sister called with a beautiful *d'var Torah*

❑ MIRACLE: Narrowly missed being hit by a truck.

❑ Son said, "Change the tape in your mind, Mommy," when I was angry.

❑ The mechanic fixed the car in an hour.

❑ MIRACLE: Happened to overhear two people in store talking about a new medication for son's illness.

❑ Holding my baby when he's asleep.

❑ Went out to eat. Had fun.

Having a very kind and caring pediatrician.

MIRACLE: Sarah, who was infertile for years, had a baby!

MIRACLE: Leah, who was single for years, got married!

Son turned off the fire just before the pot boiled over!

MIRACLE: Put my seatbelt on three minutes before the accident.

Got a parking space in the busiest part of town.

Had money to buy a full tank of gas.

MIRACLE: Got to the appointment on time despite traffic jam.

Received a thank-you note from a child!

MIRACLE: The emergency room doctor just happened to be an expert in eye problems, which saved my daughter's sight.

A neighbor happened to be going to the store and said she would get me what I wanted to save me the trip.

MIRACLE: We won the lawsuit!

Keeping a notebook is essential to your mental health. It helps you internalize the feeling that God is truly with you in your daily life and that your Godly soul can be your guide at all times. To pass this concept on to your children or grandchildren, keep a notebook for the younger ones and encourage the older ones to keep their own journal.

Each day, ask them for one item. Simply say, "What act of self-control did you do today that was really difficult for you?" "What can you thank Hashem for today?"

Children's Victories

Get a small shoe box and cut a slit in the top. During the week, write down your children's acts of kindness and self-discipline and slip the notes into the box. The children should also do this for each other and for you, too! Smaller children can ask older ones to write for them. Hand out the notes at the Shabbos table. Each child has the option of reading his note out loud or, in the case of very young children, having them read. This creates a positive atmosphere during the entire week, as everyone is looking for the good! The entire family can share a special treat as a prize for writing.

AGE 3:

❑ Got a tissue for Mommy when she sneezed.

❑ Ran and got a diaper for the baby when Mommy asked.

❑ Let the nurse give me a shot.

❑ Hugged my little sister when she was crying to make her feel better.

❑ Put away my toys in the toy box.

AGE 4:

❑ Sat in the dentist's chair.

❑ Waited calmly for Mommy by the front door when she

didn't get home on time.

❑ Went to *gan* all by myself without crying.

❑ Ate with a fork instead of with my fingers.

❑ Got into my pajamas when Mommy told me to.

❑ Got out of the bathtub when Mommy said, even though I wanted to stay.

❑ Waited patiently until Mommy finished talking on the phone.

AGE 5:

❑ Said the whole *Shema* by myself.

❑ Sat by Daddy in *shul* for a whole hour even though I wanted to go outside and play.

❑ Gave in and let younger brother have my toy.

❑ Let the guest sleep in my bed.

❑ Stopped playing and came in the house when Mommy called me.

❑ Got dressed by myself without Mommy having to scream at me.

❑ Didn't complain when I didn't get to sit where I wanted in the car.

❑ Didn't knock down the tower my little sister built with all my blocks.

❑ Didn't nag my Mommy all the time when we went to the mall. I was *mistapek b'mu'at* and was happy with just one thing.

Didn't hit brother back when he made faces at me.

Didn't scream when Mommy said she had to go out at night even though I didn't want her to go.

AGE 8:

❑ Brought Mommy the baby's pacifier when she told me to, even though I was in the middle of a computer game.

❑ Bought Mommy flowers with my allowance money.

❑ Got my things ready the night before school.

❑ Brushed my teeth without waiting for Mommy to ask if I did.

❑ "Replayed the scene" after being *chutzpadik* to Mommy.

❑ Gave in and let younger brother sit next to Daddy in *shul*.

❑ Helped guest carry suitcase into the house.

❑ Didn't return a hurt with a hurt when schoolmate insulted me.

❑ Memorized *pesukim* for a test.

❑ Didn't pull my sister's hair when she bugged me.

❑ Wanted to call brother a name, but didn't — instead I said, "Thank you for the *mitzvah*," and I felt happy!

❑ Didn't complain too much about my stomach-ache; controlled myself and didn't eat any candy for a whole day.

❑ Said, "It's Hashem's will" when I didn't get the teacher I wanted.

❑ Didn't wipe my shoes on the towel; took a rag instead.

❑ *Davened*, even though I wanted to go out and play so badly.

❑ Didn't yell at my brother for drinking from my cup.

❑ Took a tissue instead of wiping my nose on my sleeve.

AGE 10:

❑ Woke up in a bad mood but decided to smile anyway.

❑ Made a chart and gave myself stars for getting up in time.

❑ Decided not to hit my little brother any more.

❑ Gave Mommy benefit of the doubt when she was late.

❑ Invited the new girl in our class over to my house.

❑ Didn't say *lashon ha-ra* about a mean girl in my class.

❑ Did all my homework.

☐ Took out the garbage twice in one day without grumbling. Lied and said, "Thank you for the *mitzvah*" but then it was true!

☐ Didn't lie about dropping the baby; I admitted I did it.

☐ Didn't cheat on the math test.

☐ Didn't argue with Mommy when she said I couldn't go out.

☐ Didn't ignore Mommy when she called me.

☐ Didn't get angry when Mommy didn't have the food ready.

☐ Held the crying baby for a long time and walked with him.

☐ Apologized to Daddy after I misbehaved.

☐ Finally cut my nails after Mommy asked only three times.

☐ Got out of bed and brushed my teeth though I was half asleep.

AGE 12:

☐ Forgave girls who laughed at my new glasses.

☐ When my watch got lost, I said, "It's a triviality."

☐ Went to the hospital to visit a sick friend.

☐ Didn't nag my mother to throw me an expensive bas

mitzvah party.

❑ Took the baby out so Mommy could sleep.

❑ Didn't eat a second helping of cake.

❑ Cleaned up my room without giving Mommy a hard time!

❑ Helped a neighbor take all her packages up to her apartment.

❑ Was honest and admitted to Mommy that I stained my shirt.

❑ Gave *tzedakah* from my allowance — very hard!

❑ Did the dishes even though it wasn't my turn.

❑ Fasted the entire fast. Only grumbled a little.

AGE 14:

❑ Kept quiet and didn't join my friends who were gossiping about a new teacher.

❑ Didn't make a stink about not getting the bike I wanted.

❑ Shut my mouth instead of saying *ona'as devarim*.

❑ Cleaned off the dining room table even though it wasn't my turn.

❑ Took food to a sick neighbor, even though I was embarrassed.

❏ Took notes for classmate who was sick and read them to her.

❏ Babysat for a poor neighbor and refused to take any money for it.

After going to a lot of stores, compromised and got the shoes Mommy wanted; didn't complain about not getting my exact dream.

APPENDIX F:

Children's Gratefulness List: Hashem Loves Me!

The following section is especially helpful for children who tend to be grouchy. Writing reinforces the memory of positive events.

AGE 4:

❑ Had ice cream.

❑ Threw away my pacifier.

❑ Got new pair of shoes.

❑ Had a delicious chocolate bar all to myself.

❑ Went to the park with the babysitter.

❑ Daddy took me on his shoulders.

AGE 6:

❑ Got a new pair of *tzitzis*.

❑ Got four new toy cars because I sat quietly in the dentist's chair.

❑ Went swimming.

❑ Got new set of magic markers.

❑ Got to hold the new baby.

❑ Ride my bike.

AGE 8:

❑ Made my own omelette.

❑ Got a new backpack for school.

❑ Learned how to use a computer.

❑ Lost my bus ticket and a nice lady gave me money to get home.

❑ Got stickers and traded with a friend.

AGE 10:

❑ Mommy let me bake a cake all by myself!

❑ Got compliments on the cake I baked.

❑ Made my new baby brother smile.

❑ Mommy is teaching me how to sew.

❑ Got two books from Bubby for my birthday.

❑ Mommy didn't get angry when I lost my glasses; she said it was a triviality! Having a calmer Mommy!

❑ Someone called and said he had found my wallet!

❑ Having a best friend.

❑ Mommy saw my stained skirt and didn't get angry.

❑ Had a long walk with Daddy.

❑ Got to be the *chazan* for the class today.

❑ When I spilled the juice and just cleaned it up without grumbling, Daddy said, "There's a celebration in *Shamayim*."

❑ I'm happy that I managed to control myself and did not eat my sister's piece of cake that was in the fridge.

❑ Mommy listened to me when I was sad.

❑ Mommy let me go to the bank by myself to deposit money.

❑ Went to the park with all the kids.

❑ Went horseback riding.

❑ Got a prize for memorizing *pesukim*.

APPENDIX G:

From a Father:
The Miracle of the Notes

Dear Dr. Adahan,

I've always had a lot of problems with my oldest child, a five-year-old boy. I found I was constantly angry with him. Our relationship had deteriorated to the point where he would barely speak to me. One of the things that bothered me most was that he refused to say blessings over the food that he ate.

At your suggestion, I began to write him three notes a day, giving him positive reinforcement for doing things which pleased me. For example, I wrote:

You remembered the Hebrew letters we learned yesterday.

You understood very well what your teachers taught you about the weekly Torah portion.

You said a blessing over your cereal yesterday.

You shared your Lego with your little sister.

You helped Mommy clean up your room.

I read the notes to him every night before he went to sleep and then put them into an envelope. Sometimes he asked me to read all the notes that were there from previous days. He loved to hear them!

After two weeks, I saw a drastic change in my son. He began to cooperate and listen to me. The greatest change occurred in connection with food. He now happily says blessings before he eats. He is so happy to get his little notes. He asks me for notes whenever he deserves them.

Last night, he told me that he wanted me to write a note to myself! He told me to write FATHER on the outside, and on the inside to write: "You are a good father."

From being a father who was constantly critical and making demands, I am now a father who gives notes of encouragement. I see amazing results in both myself and my son.

Signed,
A Happy Father